Software Project Cost and Schedule Estimating

Best Practices

William H. Roetzheim
and
Reyna A. Beasley

13518 Jamul Dr.
Phone 800-477-6168   Local Phone
E-Mail: info@marotz.com   www.marotz.com

D1506332

To join a Prentice Hall PTR Internet mailing list,
point to: http://www.prenhall.com/mail_lists/

ISBN 0-13-682089-1

90000

9 780136 820895

A Prentice Hall Title
Upper Saddle River, NJ 07458

Library of Congress Cataloging-in-Publication Data

Roetzheim, William H., 1955–
    Software project cost and schedule estimating : best practices /
    William H. Roetzheim, Reyna A. Beasley.
        p.   cm.
    Includes bibliographical references and index.
    ISBN 0-13-682089-1
    1. Computer software—Development—Estimates.   I. Beasley, ReynaA.
    II. Title.
    OA76.76.D47R645 1997
    005.1'2—DC21   97-29163
                                                                  CIP

Editorial/production supervision: *Nicholas Radhuber*
Manufacturing manager: *Alexis Heydt*
Acquisitions editor: *Paul Becker*
Marketing manager: *Dan Rush*
Cover design: Wee Design
Cover design director: *Jerry Votta*

Prentice Hall books are widely used by corporations and government agencies
for training, marketing, and resale.
    The publisher offers discounts on this book when ordered in bulk quantities.
    For more information, contact:
    Phone: 800-382-3419
    Fax: 201-236-7141; e-mail: corpsales@prenhall.com
    or write:
    Prentice Hall PTR
    Corporate Sales Department
    One Lake St.
    Upper Saddle River, NJ 07458

Printed in the United States of America
10 9 8 7 6 5 4 3 2

ISBN 0-13-682089-1

Prentice-Hall International (UK) Limited, *London*
Prentice-Hall of Australia Pty. Limited, *Sydney*
Prentice-Hall Canada Inc., *Toronto*
Prentice-Hall Hispanoamericana, S.A., *Mexico*
Prentice-Hall of India Private Limited, *New Delhi*
Prentice-Hall of Japan, Inc., *Tokyo*
Simon & Schuster Asia Pte. Ltd., *Singapore*
Editora Prentice-Hall do Brazil, Ltda., *Rio de Janeiro*

Challenges, triumphs, warm contentment,
and giddy ecstasy—none would
exist were it not for Marianne.
                                    —W.R.

To my wonderful family and nephew Austen,
a child who loves life.
                                    —R.B.

TABLE OF CONTENTS

LIST OF FIGURES

LIST OF TABLES

PREFACE

In our experience, more projects are doomed from poor cost and schedule estimates than ever succumb to technical, political, or development team problems. Yet so few companies and individuals really understand that software estimating can be a *science*, not just an *art*. It really is possible to accurately and consistently estimate costs and schedules for a wide range of projects. I call this knowledge "Taking control of your life," because it gives you the skills you need to confidently predict the resources required to be successful, calculate realistic delivery times, and consistently deliver your projects on time and on budget. This book will show you how to become an estimating wizard.

We'll start by covering the various methods of estimating the size of a program (called *program volume*). We'll discuss the traditional measures of lines of code and function points, plus the latest work using graphical user interface (GUI) metrics and object metrics. We will also discuss both top down and bottom up estimating, two techniques that are especially valuable for smaller projects. We'll discuss how to quantify the impact of changes in the project environment (resources, development tools, and so on). You'll learn how to compute the optimal project schedule, and how to adjust the resource requirements for schedules that are other than optimal. We'll also show you how to incorporate risk and sensitivity analysis into your estimating process.

ABOUT THE AUTHORS

William H. Roetzheim has over 18 years experience in software engineering and is currently the Chief Executive Officer of Marotz, Inc., a Delphi development shop headquartered in Jamul, California. He has performed business needs analysis, cost-benefit analysis, and strategic planning work for the Arizona Department of Transportation; Los Angeles Fire Department; CoBank (the nation's largest agricultural bank), and Washington Inventory Service (one of the nation's two largest inventory management companies). He was the project director for a project that involved providing independent software cost and schedule analysis support to the California Department of Social Services (CDSS) and California Franchise Tax Board. He conducted an independent software cost, schedule and risk assessment of the California Statewide Automated Child Support System (SACSS) project. He is the author of fourteen technical books and over forty articles on various software subjects, including one on project management, one on software standards, one on software procurement, and several on system analysis and/or client-server related technical skills.

Reyna A. Beasley is a Senior Technical Analyst with Marotz, Inc. She has assisted with strategic planning, cost benefit studies, and project management of large, complex projects developed using Delphi.

chapter

SOFTWARE PROJECT COST AND SCHEDULE ESTIMATING

WHY BOTHER ESTIMATING

Whether you're working on small projects or large, you've probably seen the effect of poor cost or schedule estimates. Under estimates result in long hours, poor quality, and shattered customer expectations. Just look at some of the cost overruns identified by Robert Charette in his book, *Software Engineering Risk Analysis and Management.*[1]

Unfortunately, for all too many companies the approach to "estimating" is to use one of the following forms of non-estimating:

- Find out what the customer/manager/marketer thinks it should cost, then give that as your estimate.
- Find out how much money is available, then give that as your estimate.
- Guess; for big projects, have more than one person guess and average the results.

[1] Charette, Robert N., *Software Engineering Risk Analysis and Management.* McGraw-Hill, 1989, p. 18.

1

TABLE 1 PROJECT COST OVERRUNS

Project	Minimum cost overrun
U.S. Office of Mines	$15M
Bank of America	$65M
United Airlines Reservation System	$145M
NORAD Update	$207M
U.S. Navy Automated Financial System	$446M
Advanced Logistic System	$490M
U.S. Army TACFIRE	$525M
United Education and Software Inc.	$650M
U.S. Army Sgt. York	$1,000M
U.S. Air Force B-1B EW System	$1,200M
British Nimrod	$2,200M

- For projects you don't like, estimate a big number to kill the project.
- For projects you like, estimate a small number to get authorization to start work.

We'll give you the powerful, scientific techniques you need to confidently produce and defend an estimate and a schedule that can be realistically met, thereby saving both yourself and your company from potentially disastrous project failures.

THE ESTIMATING LIFE CYCLE

First, it is important to recognize at the macro level the limitations of software cost estimating. As shown in Figure 1, the typical accuracy of cost estimates varies based on the current software development stage. Initially, at the concept stage, you may be presented with a very vague definition of the project. Even the requirements are not yet fully understood, but the general purpose of the new software can be understood. At this point, estimates with an accuracy of ± 50% are typical for an experienced esti-

Macro life cycle:

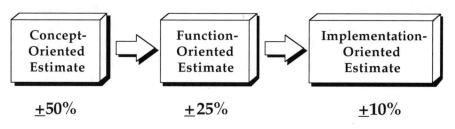

Typical Accuracies

FIGURE 1 MACRO LIFE CYCLE

mator, and informal techniques dominate (historical comparisons, group consensus, and so on). For government procurements, this level of estimating is done by the government as part of the feasibility study work. After the requirements are reasonably well understood, a function-oriented estimate can be prepared. At this point, estimates with an accuracy of ± 25% are typical for an experienced estimator, and the techniques described in these articles dominate. For government procurements, this is normally done by the contractor as part of the proposal process. Finally, after the detailed design is complete, an implementation-oriented estimate may be prepared. This estimate is typically accurate within ± 10%. The object metric techniques described in these articles are particularly appropriate at this point, and the project estimates can often be refined based on a better understanding of the problem being solved and the development environment itself.

One common concern is that many projects are forced to live within the original budget even when later estimates show it was incorrect. The feeling is often, "Why bother re-estimating when the budget can't change anyway?" We point out that software, to a large extent, varies with respect to the features you design into the program. If you become aware of a project scope problem early in the lifecycle, you can always work to adjust features to better meet the original estimates. The key is to recognize the importance of periodic re-estimates throughout the project lifecycle, thereby identifying problems early, while you have an opportunity to take corrective action.

Whether you're preparing the concept-, function-, or implementation-oriented estimate, the micro lifecycle steps are the same. As shown in Figure 2, you begin by estimating the program volume. This can be accomplished using estimates of the number of lines of code, function points, GUI metrics, or object metrics. You then select and apply coefficients to calculate an unadjusted estimate of the level of effort. This is the value that would apply if this project was totally typical in every way. Project-specific adjustments are then incorporated. Finally, adjustments are added to provide for schedules that deviate from the optimal schedule. Each of these steps is covered in detail during the remainder of this discussion. The typical outputs of an estimating task include life-cycle costs (maintenance and support costs); a staffing profile; cost broken down by phase; cost broken down by activity; estimated page counts for documents; and a project risk profile.

In the next chapter, we jump into the process of quantifying the volume of a software program.

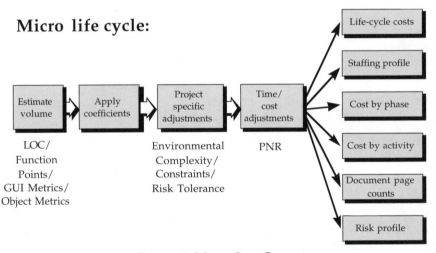

FIGURE 2 MICRO LIFE CYCLE

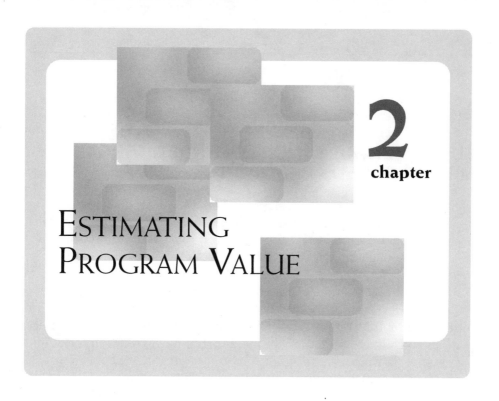

2
chapter

ESTIMATING PROGRAM VALUE

The first step in preparing an estimate is to develop an estimate of the program volume. There are six common approaches to meeting this objective.

1. Lines of code,
2. Function points,
3. GUI metrics,
4. Object metrics,
5. Bottom up, and
6. Top down.

For small projects (generally, less than $50K), you will probably exclusively use either a bottom up or top down estimate as your volume estimate. For medium-sized projects ($50K to $1M), you will probably use one of the metric-based approaches (lines-of-code, function points, GUI metrics, or object metrics) and supplement this estimate with one of the two heuristic approaches (bottom up or top down) to validate the numbers. For larger projects, you'll probably want to use two or more of the metric-based approaches and correlate the results as your primary volume estimating methodology.

FUNDAMENTAL CONCEPTS UNDERLYING METRIC-BASED APPROACHES

Metric-based volume estimates use a metric that is available early in the life cycle to predict effort during the entire life cycle. The original metric-based approach used lines of code and was popularized by the Constructive Cost Model, or COCOMO. The basic COCOMO model has been incorporated into literally dozens of costing tools, and remains the most common approach. Lines of code are particularly valuable for real-time and embedded systems with little user interface. Function points were introduced by IBM in the early 1980s. This approach uses user-interface features to estimate program volume. It is the most common technique for estimating management information system (MIS) application volume. GUI metrics, introduced in the early 1990s, are similar to function points but use graphical user interface features to predict application volume. Finally, object metrics have become feasible only with the popularization of object-oriented development and use objects as a predictor of program volume.

You will find that all metric-based approaches work somewhat similarly, in that the analyst is asked to enter a best, expected, and worst case estimate of the metric being used. For example, in a selected program module, you might feel that it is possible to complete the task with 5,000 lines of code (best case); you believe that it will probably take 8,000 lines of code (expected case); and you're completely certain that it can be done with no more than 12,000 lines of code (worst case). The mean and standard deviation can then be calculated as follows.

> Mean = (best + worst + (4 * expected)) / 6
>
> Standard deviation = (worst − best) / 6

The mean is the number that should statistically be too high 50% of the time and too low 50% of the time. The standard deviation measures how much deviation you can expect in the final number. For example, if you take the mean plus three times the standard deviation, there is a 99% probability that the project will come in *under* your estimate.

Estimating Lines-of-Code

Lines-of-code is the oldest, most widely used, and most widely lambasted of the volume metrics. First popularized by Barry Boehm in his Constructive Cost Model, it has become the basis for a vast array of software cost estimating tools. Although other techniques have made major inroads in the world of MIS applications, lines-of-code is still the standard for applications with a lot of behind-the-scenes processing. This includes system programming, embedded programming, and most scientific programming. Even in the MIS world, it remains popular as a technique for many code intensive applications.

Opponents of lines-of-code argue that counting rules cause lines-of-code counts to vary wildly. For example, they point out, whether or not to include comments can impact the apparent size of a program by a factor of two. In fact, however, standard line counting rules have become widely accepted. Comments do not count; blank lines do not count; code that is included numerous times (e.g., include files) counts only the first time it is included; standard operating system include files do not count. Code lines count; job control lines count; user defined include files count (once); and SQL statements count. A line of code is defined as a logical line, but it is not necessarily a physical line. For example, in C and C++, it is common to count the number of semicolons to determine the line count. In this manner, placing three logical statements on one physical line still counts as three lines of code.

Another compelling series of arguments against lines-of-code revolves around the fact that the delivered functionality per line of code will vary based on the language being used. We believe that this argument dooms lines-of-code as an effective measure of programmer productivity, and we strongly discourage companies from measuring programmer performance using lines-of-code developed as a metric. On the other hand, the use of lines-of-code as a predictor of total project effort continues to be successful for a wide range of programming projects using a variety of languages.

Defining Modules

When estimating the number of lines of code, you begin by breaking the project into a series of modules that you can independently estimate. To determine the total count of the lines-of-code, add all of the line counts for these individual modules. By breaking the project into modules prior to estimating the line counts, you gain several advantages:

- Individual modules will often be similar to modules developed as part of previous projects, leading to more accurate estimates based on historic comparisons.
- Individual modules will often be developed by one individual or a small team, so each person or group can estimate the lines for the individual modules that they will be responsible for developing.
- The process of decomposing the project into modules helps to ensure that no major functional areas are left out of the estimate.

Questions may arise regarding the definition of a program module from an estimating perspective. For procedural languages, a module will normally equate to a single source code file (perhaps with an associated header definition file) that compiles to an object file as part of the software building process. For object-oriented development projects, many companies have guidelines which require each object to be contained in its own individual file, even if the object's code is small. If this is the case, then a module may be better defined as a collection of objects (or in C++, classes) that are related via inheritance.

Installing Cost•Xpert on Your Machine

We're going to walk through the process of entering software volume estimates into a typical software costing tool, Cost•Xpert. To get the maximum benefit from this book, you should follow along in the tool as we walk through the examples. Of course, this requires that you install the working demonstration copy of the software that was bound into the book; you can also download it from *www.marotz.com*.

Closing Applications Before Installing   Prior to installing Cost•Xpert, it is best if you close other running applications. This will free as much memory as possible for use by the installation program, thus minimizing the possibility of an "out of memory" condition. If the installation program still does not run properly, you may wish to exit Windows, then restart Windows. This will free any resources, including memory, that other applications may have left allocated.

CD-ROM Contents The CD-ROM accompanying this book contains a demonstration copy of Cost•Xpert, Risk•Xpert, Strategy•Xpert, and HTSO. These programs are further described in the Appendices to this book.

Checking the Readme File The first installation disk contains a text file called README.TXT. This file contains information and answers to questions that were too new for inclusion in the hard copy documentation. This file will automatically be displayed at the conclusion of your software installation. If you are having problems getting Cost•Xpert to install on your system, you should use a text editor (e.g., Notepad) to view this file to see if your particular problem is covered.

What the Installation Program Does First, unlike many other Windows programs, the Cost•Xpert installation program *does not* make changes to your system configuration files or modify your initialization (.ini) files. Later in this section, we describe the exact directories that the installation program creates, and the files that the installation program places in those directories. No other changes are made to your system during installation. Deleting Cost•Xpert from your system is as simple as deleting the indicated directories.

Insert the Cost•Xpert distribution CD-ROM into your computer's CD-ROM drive slot. Change directories to the Cost•Xpert directory and run the setup program.

Customizing the Installation You may want to configure your system to choose between installing only the Cost•Xpert application or the application plus the empty data files. You will want to keep this in mind when you are doing a reinstallation of the application and you do not want to overwrite your existing data files. To do this, choose the Custom Setup from the install disk and check the box that contains Application only (the check box for Empty Data Files needs to be blank, otherwise new data files will be installed and overwrite existing data files).

Completing the Installation After you have selected your configuration, SETUP will complete the installation. In addition to copying files from the disk to your hard drive, SETUP will create a Cost•Xpert program group and install the Cost•Xpert application icon in this program group. At the conclusion of the installation process, the Cost•Xpert readme file will be displayed. Read this file carefully for any new information about the Cost•Xpert application.

Loading the Sample Project

A project called "Sample – 3D Automation" is included as part of the installation procedure, and all of the examples in this book are based on that project. You may want to open that project when following along with our examples so that your screens will match those in this book. Of course, you should feel free to explore the tool by changing the sample project to your heart's content!

To begin running Cost•Xpert, double click on the program icon as displayed in Figure 3.

FIGURE 3 COST•XPERT ICON

After running Cost•Xpert and loading the "Sample – 3D Automation" project, your initial screen will look like Figure 4. In the following chapter, we'll cover all of these project characteristics in detail; but for now, let's click on the Volume notebook tab to look at how we enter volume estimates.

Entering Estimates for Lines-of-Code

The volume tab for the Sample project is shown in Figure 5. As you can see, there are subtabs for each of the different approaches of measuring program volume. We will cover each of these in the remainder of this chapter, but for now, let's focus on the estimate in terms of source lines-of-code (SLOC).

Notice the radio buttons at the top of the tab labeled *New* and *Reused*. We will be discussing how to deal with software reuse in your

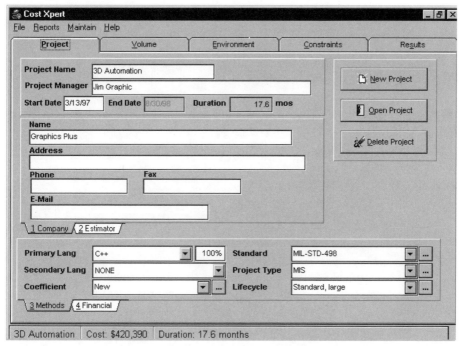

FIGURE 4 INITIAL SCREEN, SAMPLE PROJECT

volume estimates later in this chapter, so for now, just be sure that the *New* radio button is selected.

In the grid, you can enter each of the program modules along with your best case, expected case, and worst case estimates of the number of lines of code for each. The program calculates the mean and standard deviation using the formulas given earlier in this chapter.

Viewing the Initial Results

As you enter the modules, the total calculated cost and duration is shown on the bottom of the notebook. These numbers will change significantly as we complete the estimating process, so don't rely on them too heavily until you near the end of your estimate. They are especially useful, however, when working in a design to cost mode. After you

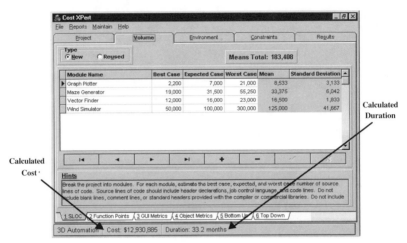

FIGURE 5 CALCULATED COST AND CALCULATED DURATION

develop your initial estimate, with all of the "bells and whistles" included, and you enter the correct values for environmental variables, constraints, and so on (all covered later in this book), you can view the final cost. If the cost is too high, you make adjustments to delivered functionality, schedule, and so on until the cost is within the desired range. This will then define the functionality and schedule which you can comfortably commit to deliver within the available funds.

Estimating Function Points

Function points were first proposed by Albrecht as a measure of program volume while he was with IBM. The idea is simple. The program's delivered functionality (and hence, cost) can be measured by the number of ways it must interact with the users. The specifications for this user interaction can normally be estimated early in the software life cycle.

To determine the number of function points, you estimate the number of external inputs, external interface files, external outputs, external queries, and logical internal tables. *External inputs* are data entry screens or dialogs. *External interface files* are files that this system creates for use by other applications, and files that other systems create for input into this application. *External outputs* are reports and read-only query screens.

External queries are on-line transactions from other systems that must be handled by this system. *Logical internal tables* are the relational tables or other storage files used by the system.

As with all of the metric-oriented estimates, you estimate each value in terms of a best case, expected case, and worst case estimate to allow the mean and standard deviation to be calculated. Figure 6 illustrates this for our Sample application in Cost●Xpert.

Function-point-based estimates are one of the best approaches for MIS applications that have a significant interaction with the environment, especially when this environmental interaction is the major cost driver. They are the dominant form of estimating in industries such as banking. In addition, they are one of the few metrics that seem to be an effective measure of programmer productivity while developing this type of application. Unfortunately, they are significantly less effective (and

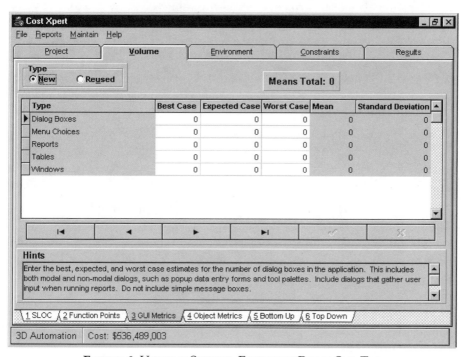

FIGURE 6 VOLUME SCREEN, FUNCTION POINT SUB-TAB

correspondingly less popular) for applications where the environmental interactions are secondary to the algorithmic requirements of the program. For example, it is easy to imagine a program that calculates the burst pressure of a pipeline using a single file as an input and a single number as an output, yet it is very complicated and difficult to write. As another example, an embedded flight control system that has almost no environmental interaction is obviously quite expensive to develop.

Although function point fans have extended the concept to support feature points (which are basically measures of internal algorithmic complexity), most estimators working outside the domain of function points prefer to fall back on source lines-of-code, or perhaps use object metrics (covered later in this chapter).

Estimating GUI Metrics

GUI (Graphical User Interface) metrics are relatively new to the cost estimating scene. First proposed in 1993 by Roetzheim (then with Booz, Allen & Hamilton), they are designed specifically for estimating the client side of client-server development projects using the various GUI development tools. GUI metrics have been used successfully on approximately 25 projects to our knowledge; and they were the subject of a PhD thesis that concluded that they were effective in the target environment.

Similar in concept to function points, GUI metrics measure interaction with the environment and the system's users. This interaction is expressed in terms of dialog boxes, menu choices, reports, tables, and windows.

Dialog boxes include both modal and non-modal dialog boxes such as popup data entry forms and tool palettes. Dialogs that gather user input in preparation for running reports are also included. Simple message boxes are not included, although they are technically a form of dialog box.

Menu choices include the number of unique menu choices in the application. Menu choices that simply display a lower level menu do not count. Menu choices that appear in multiple places (e.g., on multiple menus) but perform exactly the same function are only counted once.

Reports include system reports. In some cases, a single report will combine a wide variety of dissimilar data into one report (often a form).

For example, I once worked on an application where the final output was a single 20-page report containing a wide variety of data, including vehicle information, driver information, building descriptions, loss history, and so on. In this case, each collection of related data should be considered one report.

Tables include the number of logical relational tables in the system, and should be identical to the number of tables in function point estimates.

Windows include the number of independent windows in the system. For a single document interface (SDI) application, this will normally be 1. For a multiple document interface (MDI) application, this will normally be the number of unique child window types plus one for the main frame window.

Figure 7 shows the data entry screen in Cost•Xpert for entering GUI metric volume estimates.

Estimating Object Metrics

Object-metric-based estimating is becoming popular among companies using object-oriented techniques throughout the software life cycle (e.g., object-oriented analysis, design, and programming). Although still relatively new, it was applied on a massive scale within Hewlett Packard with great success and we have personally used it successfully on perhaps a dozen projects. One very nice thing about the object-metric approach is that it works equally well with both the MIS type applications and with the embedded, scientific, and system-level programming projects that are not well served by either function points or GUI metrics. Of course, a disadvantage is that it only works if you are using the object-oriented techniques.

In a nutshell, object metrics involve estimating the size of the application in terms of the number of objects that will be required to deliver the desired functionality. Early versions involved estimating the effort in terms of object exclusively. We prefer a hybrid where the number of tables and reports (which are often implemented without the use of objects) are also factored into the equation. Thus, an object metric volume estimate consists of the number of objects, the number of tables, and the number of reports. This approach is illustrated in Figure 8.

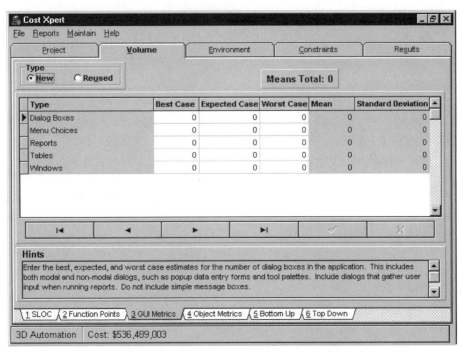

FIGURE 7 VOLUME SCREEN, GUI METRICS SUB-TAB

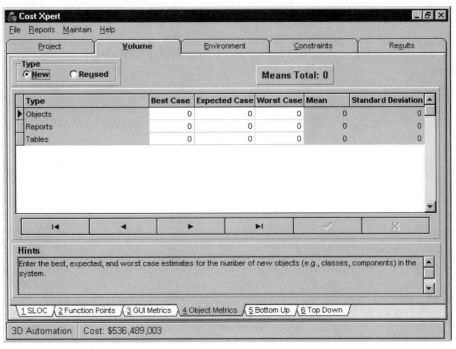

FIGURE 8 VOLUME SCREEN, OBJECT METRICS SUB-TAB

Each of these approaches to estimating a program's volume involves estimating some aspect of the program, a metric, that we believe is directly correlated with the ultimate program size. We discussed the use of lines-of-code, function points, GUI metrics, and object metrics. In the next section, we discuss estimating the program size directly using heuristic approaches.

FUNDAMENTAL CONCEPTS UNDERLYING HEURISTIC APPROACHES

Heuristic is another word for "rule of thumb." Metric-based approaches rely on a correlation between the metric being employed and the ultimate effort involved in building the software. The relationship between this metric and the ultimate cost is not necessarily simple or linear (and in fact, we will see that it is typically not linear), but the correlation exists nevertheless. Heuristic approaches to estimating the program volume rely on the fact that the same basic activities will be required for a typical software development project and that these activities will require a predictable percentage of the overall effort. For example, small traditional projects typically include activities that can be categorized as requirements analysis, design, coding, testing, and documentation. The percentage of effort required for these activities is predictable, but may vary based on the type of project and the size of the project. This knowledge is the basis of heuristic-based estimating.

Bottom Up

For people with little or no training in software cost estimating, bottom up cost estimating is typically the approach used. The basic concept is simple.

Divide the program into modules (using the same approach followed when estimating using lines-of-code). For each module, directly estimate the level of effort required in terms of person months or person hours. This tells you the estimated total effort for the coding portion of the development. Quite often, this portion of the estimate relies heavily on input from the actual programming team. In general, programmers are much better at estimating programming time than they are at estimating the time required for other software life-cycle activities such as design and testing.

Now, look at the other life-cycle activities that are required. This list of activities will vary based on the life cycle being used during the development effort; in addition, there may be some project-specific activities. For each of these activities, estimate the effort required.

Finally, compare the percentages of effort for each activity in your project plan with standard percentages. If your percentages roughly match the standard percentages, then you can be relatively confident that your allocation of effort between activities is reasonable. If your percentages deviate from the standard percentages significantly, this may indicate an unreasonable amount of effort, either too high or too low, for one or more activities.

Figure 9 illustrates this approach. In the Code grid, you define your coding activities and enter a best case, expected case, and worst case estimate of the level of effort required to code the indicated modules. In the Activities grid, you define the project activities if they vary from the defaults for the selected life cycle; then you enter a best case, expected case, and worst case estimate of the level of effort required for each activity. The actual percentages and typical percentages applied to each activity are also shown in this grid.

For bottom up cost estimating, you start with a list of all required activities, estimate the effort for each, compare these estimates with typical percentages, then add the costs to a total project cost. Top down cost estimating, which is covered next, takes pretty much the opposite approach.

Top Down

For top down cost estimating, you begin with an estimate of the total effort for the entire project. You then use typical percentages for each life-cycle activity to calculate the effort for each of those activities. You can then compare the predicted effort for each activity with the required work to determine if the numbers seem reasonable. If not, the total effort can be adjusted up or down as required. Figure 10 illustrates this concept.

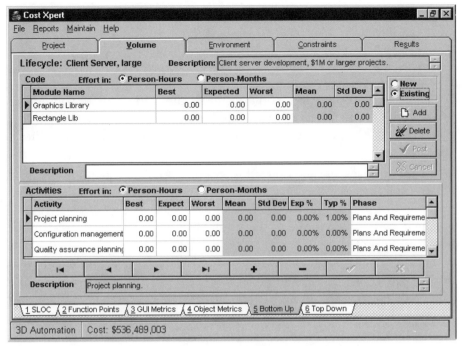

FIGURE 9 VOLUME SCREEN, BOTTOM UP SUB-TAB

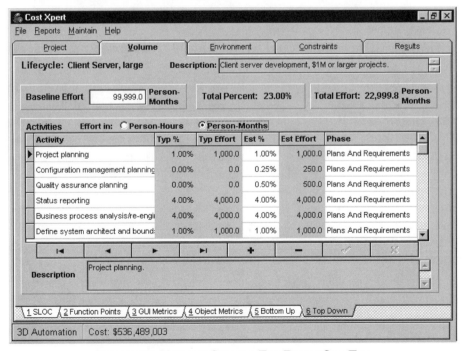

FIGURE 10 VOLUME SCREEN, TOP DOWN SUB-TAB

The Delphi Technique

For each of the techniques, you are still required to estimate something. Whether it's source lines-of-code, number of data entry screens, objects, or actual effort required—the raw numbers still need to come from somewhere.

In many cases, either you or the senior technical individuals involved will be able to provide the required input. For example, the systems analyst will normally be the best judge of objects; the business analyst will normally be the best judge of the number of data entry screens; and the senior programmer will normally be the best judge of lines-of-code or actual coding effort required. For projects where you simply cannot have even a small mistake, you might want to consider improving these raw estimates using something called the Delphi technique.

The Delphi technique is a group decision-making technique that often results in better estimates when time and money warrant the extra effort. The concept is simple. You get multiple "experts" to estimate the same item, then compare the results. If the results are within an acceptable error tolerance, you go with the average. If the results are not within the acceptable error tolerance, you have two choices.

The fastest approach is to have the experts involved sit down together and discuss the reasons for their discrepancies. This is known as the *accelerated Delphi technique.* They hammer out any issues, learn from each other's experience, and keep voting. Eventually they arrive at a consensus. This approach is the fastest because the communication between team members is very fast and efficient. The problem develops when one or more team members are dominant over the others. This dominance may be related to perceived technical authority (e.g., the senior programmer with more technical experience intimidates the less experienced individuals); positional authority (e.g., the department head intimidates the analysts); or personality (e.g., the aggressive individual dominates the more meek individuals). If any of these factors is a potential problem, then the traditional Delphi technique is your best bet.

In the *traditional Delphi technique,* great pains are taken to foster anonymity among the individuals providing input. One very effective way to make this happen is to take advantage of e-mail. Each participant mails an estimate to a single facilitator responsible for collecting the input data. For areas where there is a significant discrepancy, the facilitator then notifies all participants of the discrepancy via e-mail. Each individual then provides the logic behind the estimate to the facilitator. The facilitator sanitizes these inputs by removing names and ensuring that all inputs are equivalent with respect to grammar, vocabulary, and so on. The consolidated inputs are then mailed to each individual. They vote and mail their responses to the facilitator, and the process repeats until a consensus is reached.

If you can afford the time and effort, the Delphi technique is very effective in improving the quality of the input data in your estimating process, and hence improving the quality of your estimates. In addition to applying this approach to volume measures for new code, you can apply the technique to change estimates for reused code. The subject of dealing with code reuse in general is the topic of our next section.

DEALING WITH CODE REUSE

Reuse of code, objects, or even entire applications is becoming de rigueur for all software projects. So of course, our method of estimating program volume must provide a means of estimating the costs associated with reuse of code. To do this, you start by actually counting the value being measured in the existing application(s). For example, if you are using lines-of-code, you would use a code counting utility to physically count the lines of code in the existing program modules. If you are using function points, you count the existing reports, screens, tables, and so on.

Calculating the Equivalent Volume

Our goal is to use the known value for the volume of reusable code to determine the equivalent volume of new code. Think about it this way. If we have 100 function points worth of reusable code, but the reusable code is completely useless, then it won't save us any effort at all; thus the equivalent amount of new code is 100 function points. If we have 100 function points worth of reusable code and we can reuse it without any changes, re-testing, or integration whatsoever, then the equivalent amount of new code is 0 function points. If we have 100 function points worth of reusable code and this saves us half the effort relative to new code, then the equivalent amount of new code is 50 function points.

We convert from reused volume values to equivalent new volume values by looking at three factors: Percent Design Modification, Percent Code Modification, and Percent Integration and Test.

Percent Design Modification measures how much design effort will be saved by the reused code. A value of 0% says that the reused code is perfectly designed for the new application and no design time will be required at all. A value of 100% says that the design is totally wrong and the existing design won't save us any time at all. A value of 50% says that the design will require some changes and that the effort involved in making these changes is 50% of the effort of doing the design from scratch. For typical software reuse, the Percent Design Modification will vary from 50% to 80%. If the number was below 50%, we would probably consider the existing code to be too different for us to get much value.

Percent Code Modification measures how much coding and unit testing effort will be saved by the reused code. A value of 0% says that the reused code is perfectly written for the new application and no coding or unit testing will be required at all. If the reused code was developed in a different language and you need to translate the code to your current language, the value would be 100%. Numbers in between imply varying amounts of code reuse. The Percent Code Modification should always be equivalent to or higher than the Percent Design Modification. As a rule of thumb, we find that the Percent Code Modification is 20% higher than the Percent Design Modification.

Percent Integration and Test measures how much integration and testing effort will be saved by the reused code. A value of 0% means that you did not anticipate any integration or integration test effort at all. A value of 100% says that you plan to spend just as much time integrating and testing the code as you would if it was developed as part of this project. The Percent Integration and Test should always be equivalent to or higher than the Percent Code Modification. It is not unusual for this factor to be 100%, especially for mission-critical systems where the risk of failure is significant. For commercial off-the-shelf components (purchased libraries) where the Percent Design Modification and Percent Code Modification are often zero, it is not unusual to see a value of 50% for Percent Integration and Test; this allows for the learning curve, integration effort, and time spent testing the application with the commercial component.

Finally, after you have measured your existing code's volume and estimated your Percent Design Modification (DM), Percent Code Modification (CM), and Percent Integration and Test (I&T) for this existing code, you are ready to calculate the equivalent volume of new code (EV) as follows:

$$EV = (.4\ DM) + (.3\ CM) + (.3\ I\&T)$$

Figure 11 shows the grid used to enter this data into Cost•Xpert. In this sample screen, we are looking at software reuse in terms of lines-of-code. The screens for function points, GUI metrics, and object metrics are conceptually identical. To access this screen, you simply select the *Reused* radio button at the top of the screen.

Reuse in an Object-Oriented Environment

The situation becomes a bit more interesting when dealing with the reuse of objects in an object-oriented development environment. The true strength of object-oriented programming is the use of inheritance to easily reuse and extend code. But how do you estimate the cost savings associated with this reuse? We have found that a simplistic approach gives good results.

If you are reusing an object from an internal or commercial library without any changes, consider it a freebie. Of course, we all know that there is a learning curve associated with the reuse of these objects, but we have found that this can be safely ignored if you are confident that objects are stable and do what you need.

If you need to change an object in some way, then reuse it exactly as you would reuse other items, estimating the Percent Design Modification, Percent Code Modification, Percent Integration and Test, and so on.

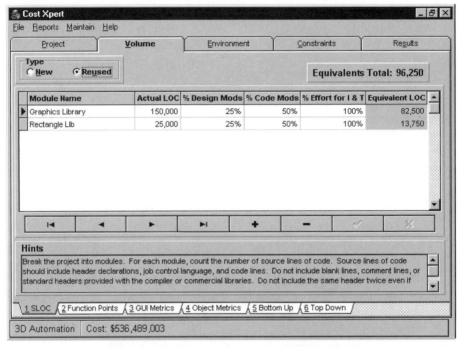

FIGURE 11 VOLUME SCREEN, SLOC SUB-TAB

If you are reusing an object through inheritance treat the parent object as a freebie and treat the child object as new code.

When you are finished, you will normally have created more than one cost estimate for your project. In fact, you could theoretically have six completely different volume estimates for the same project:

1. One based on source lines-of-code;
2. One based on function points;
3. One based on GUI metrics;
4. One based on object metrics
5. One based on a bottom up estimate; and
6. One based on a top down estimate.

As a rule of thumb, any project over $50K to $100K in size should probably be estimated using one of the heuristic methods (top down or bottom up) and one of the metric-based methods (lines-of-code, function points, GUI metrics, or object metrics). For projects over $1M, you will often want to use two of the metric-based methods plus one of the heuristic methods. Unfortunately, it would be very rare for the different methods to yield exactly the same result! How you should handle this issue is the topic of our next section.

CORRELATING THE RESULTS

When you estimate your costs using more than one estimating methodology, you will almost certainly have two different resultant cost and schedule estimates to reconcile. In Figure 12, a typical set of results is shown (actually it would be rare to estimate using all six methodologies for a single project). The first thing you want to consider is the relative discrepancies between the estimates. If they vary wildly, I would be skeptical of the overall accuracy of your estimate and go back to your original data collection to resolve the discrepancies. We look for the numbers to be within roughly 25% of each other.

You will sometimes have a valid reason to adjust the estimates either up or down. For example, historical results within your company might show that your programmers are able to deliver 20% more functionality than expected, so you can reduce your function point estimates by 20%. These adjustments can be made by entering a plus or minus value in the adjustment column. Adjustments should be the exception rather than the rule, however.

Finally, for the purpose of our final reports, we need to narrow the results down to a single estimate. There are basically three approaches to doing this:

1. Select the estimating methodology in which you have the most confidence and include that. Use each of the other estimates as a cross-check, but do not include their numbers in the final report.
2. Select each of the estimating methodologies with which you have confidence, or that seem in-line with each other, and use the average of their values. Use other estimates and "out riders" as a cross-check, but do not include their numbers in the final report.

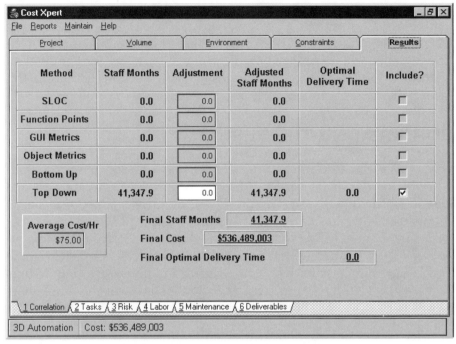

FIGURE 12 RESULTS TAB, CORRELATION SUB-TAB

3. Use the average of all estimates.

In Cost•Xpert, on the Correlation sub-tab of the Results notebook tab, you can specify which estimates you want to average together for the final numbers used for reporting purposes. Cost•Xpert calculates and displays the final, averaged effort estimate, the final cost estimate, and the optimal schedule.

In this chapter, we've discussed how to estimate your project's volume in terms of some combination of four metrics (lines-of-code, function points, GUI metrics, or object metrics) and two heuristic approaches (bottom up and top down). We covered how to deal with reused code in preparing your estimate. Finally, we described how to adjust and correlate the various volume estimates to arrive at a final estimate of the program's volume.

The mechanism used to convert from volume information to effort and schedule was not discussed at all, nor did we describe where you get those standard activities used for top down and bottom up estimating. These items are two of the topics covered in the following chapter.

3

chapter

Defining Your Project

This chapter discusses the process of setting up a project, including the project identification data, language, coefficients, software development standards, project type, and life cycle. We covered the project volume estimates prior to covering the process of defining a project; this will ensure a better understanding of some of the project-descriptive data that needs to be defined at this point.

PROJECT IDENTIFICATION DATA

Figure 13 shows the Cost•Xpert initial screen where you record project descriptive data. To create a new project, you need to enter a project name and a start date. You should also enter the name of the project manager, if assigned. The system will calculate and update the duration and end date as you work on your estimate. You also record the estimator information, and the company data at this time.

At the bottom of the page, enter additional project-definition information. Let's start with the Financial sub-tab (Figure 14). This sub-tab is used to enter the average trip cost, the average total cost per hour for staff, the inflation factor, the anticipated number of users of the applica-

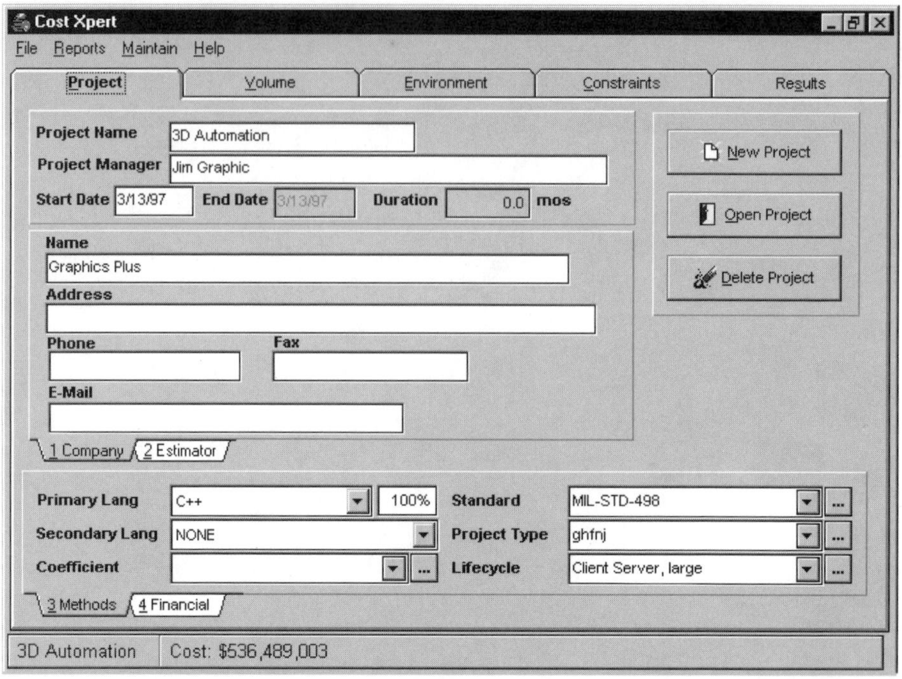

FIGURE 13 INITIAL PROJECT SCREEN

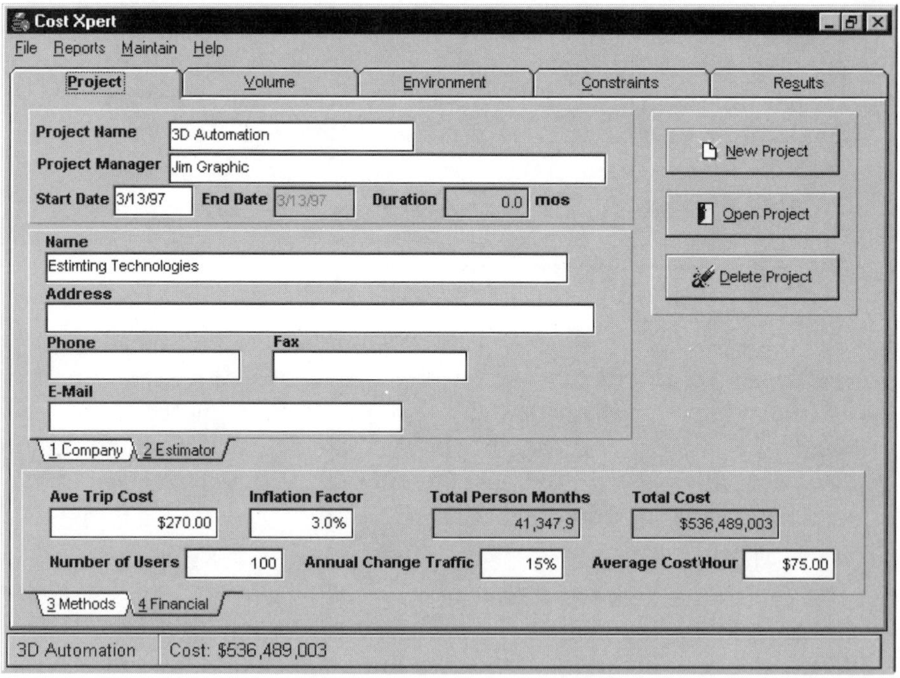

FIGURE 14 PROJECT TAB, FINANCIAL SUB-TAB

tion, and the annual change traffic. The average total cost per hour and average trip cost are used in the calculation of total project cost. The inflation factor is used when calculating life-cycle costs for software maintenance. The anticipated number of users is used in the calculation of anticipated support calls per year. Finally, the annual change traffic is used when calculating maintenance effort. These factors are discussed in more detail in later chapters

The Methods sub-tab (Figure 15) defines project descriptive information. On this sub-tab, enter the primary and secondary language, the project coefficient, the development standard that is used, the project type, and the development life cycle. For many of these, you may also press the edit button next to the combo box to modify or tailor the values. Each of these areas will be addressed individually in the sections that follow.

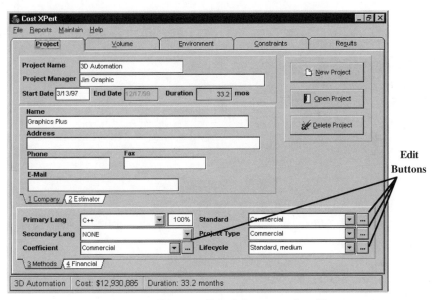

FIGURE 15 PROJECT TAB, METHODS SUB-TAB

SELECTING A PRIMARY AND SECONDARY LANGUAGE

You must enter a primary development language for the project, and you may enter a secondary language. The primary language is the development language that is used for the bulk of the code. The secondary language is the development language that is used to extend the capabilities of the primary language or is used for specific functions within the application. For example, the primary language might be Ada with C++ as the secondary language.

Your selection of a primary and secondary language significantly impacts the speed with which your programmers can deliver a specified amount of functionality. Table 2 shows the correlation between function points (a language-independent measure of functionality) and lines-of-code.

Figure 16 shows the dialog box that you can use to edit the available languages and the relationship between functionality and lines-of-code.

SELECTING A COEFFICIENT

You need to select a project coefficient to use when converting from the program volume to the total effort and optimal schedule. The meaning behind the coefficients, as well as the tailoring of the coefficients, is the subject of a later chapter. Some common coefficients you may select include:

- Commercial—commercial development projects.
- Embedded, Average—embedded, real time applications of average size and complexity.
- Embedded, Complex—embedded, real time applications that are unusually large or complex.
- Embedded, Simple—embedded, real time applications that are small and simple.
- MIS—management information systems projects that are user interface intensive and database oriented.
- Military, Ada—military projects developed using Ada.

TABLE 2 CORRELATION BETWEEN FUNCTION POINTS AND LOC

Programming language	Lines of code per function point
Smalltalk	21
C++	26
Object Pascal	29
APL	32
4GL	40
Logo	53
Basic	64
Forth	64
Lisp	64
Prolog	64
Ada	71
PL/1	80
RPG	80
Pascal	91
Algol	106
Cobol	106
Fortran	106
Jovial	106
C	150
Assembler	213

- Military, Average—military projects, typically developed to one of the military standards (e.g., DOD-STD-2167A or MIL-STD-498) and of average size and complexity.
- Military, Complex—military projects, typically developed to one of the military standards (e.g., DOD-STD-2167A or MIL-STD-498) and of unusually large size or high complexity.

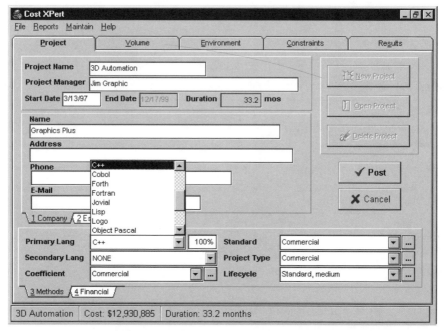

FIGURE 16 MAINTAIN LANGUAGES DIALOG BOX

- Military, Simple—military projects, typically developed to one of the military standards (e.g., DOD-STD-2167A or MIL-STD-498) and both small and simple.
- Systems—systems development projects, including operating system development, telecommunication systems, network protocols, and so on.

SELECTING A SOFTWARE DEVELOPMENT STANDARD

You can select one of the predefined software standards, or you can define your own company standard. The predefined standards include:

- Commercial—Typically used on commercial projects, especially client-server or MIS type applications.

- DOD-STD-2167A—Used on many existing military software development projects.
- IEEE—Typically used on medium to large commercial or state government projects where a degree of rigor is required, but the costs of the military standards cannot be justified. Examples include software controlling trains, medical software, and software for prison or police systems.
- MIL-STD-498—A newer military standard intended to replace DOD-STD-2167A.

The following paragraphs describe the specific documents that are included in each of the standards.

Commercial

TABLE 3 DOCUMENTS INCLUDED IN COMMERCIAL STANDARD

Title	Description
System Architecture Specification	Defines the high-level architecture of the system, including identification of internal and external systems, hardware specifications, connectivity specifications, and core decisions about the development environment. The development environment might include the DBMS, operating system, network protocols, and development language and tools.
Software Requirement Specification	Documentation of the essential requirements (functions, performance, design constraints, and attributes) of the software and its external interfaces.
General System Design	A representation of software created to facilitate analysis, planning, implementation, and decision making. The software design description is used as a medium for communicating software design information, and may be considered a blueprint or model of the system. As a minimum, most commercial General System Designs include a representation of the user interface, the database design, the report specifications, and some representation of the system's modules or components.

continued

TABLE 3 DOCUMENTS INCLUDED IN COMMERCIAL STANDARD *(continued)*

Title	Description
Detailed System Design	For small projects, a detailed system design may only be prepared for specific components that are complex. For large projects, the Detailed System Design is used to provide specific implementation guidance to the programmers. It may consist of pseudocode, detailed definitions of object structure, data flow diagrams, truth tables, or any other mechanism suitable to the problem at hand.
Software Development Plan	A software project development plan is the controlling document for managing a software project; it defines the technical and managerial processes necessary to satisfy the project requirements.
Product Description	The product description identifies the variations of the product that will be sold (single user, client-server, demo, etc.) and identifies the key features and benefits of each. It is used by the developers and by the marketing department to identify the variations of the software that must be created.
Software Test Plan	The Software Test Plan describes the software test environment, test resources required, and test schedule.
Test Cases	The test cases define the specific items to be tested (test cases) along with required documentation of the required data structures and test scripts.
Test Results	The test results describe the results of the testing and provide recommendations about the product.
User's Manual	The user's manual offers user documentation of program function.
System Operations Plan	The system operations plan defines operational procedures for the software, including installation, backup, recovery, security, support, troubleshooting, problem reporting procedures, and so on.

DOD-STD-2167A

TABLE 4 DOCUMENTS INCLUDED IN DOD-STD-2167A STANDARD

Title	Description
Software Development Plan (SDP)	The Software Development Plan describes the contractor's plans for conducting software development and is used by the government to monitor the procedures, management, and contract work effort of the contractor(s) performing software development.
System Segment Specification (SSS)	The System Segment Specification specifies the requirements for a system or a segment. These requirements then become the Functional Baseline for the system or segment. The System Segment Specification is also used to provide an overview of the system or segment to training personnel, support personnel, or users of the system.
System Segment Design Document (SSDD)	The System Segment Design Document describes the decomposition of the system segment into Hardware Configuration Items (HWCIs), Computer Software Configuration Items (CSCIs), and manual operations. This information is then used as the basis for developing the various requirements specifications for each HWCI and CSCI.
Software Requirement Specification (SRS)	The Software Requirements Specification for a CSCI may contain several requirements all designed to satisfy a single requirement in the System Segment Specification.
Interface Requirement Specification (IRS)	The detailed requirements for interfaces between each CSCI and other HWCIs/CSCIs is described in the Interface Requirements Specification(s).
Preliminary Software Design Document (SDD)	This document includes the functional decomposition of the CSCI requirements into Computer Software Components (CSCs) and Computer Software Units (CSUs) and the allocation of CSCI requirements to CSCs and CSUs.
Final Software Design Document (SDD)	This document contains the detailed design of the CSCI software to meet the allocated requirements.

continued

Title	Description
Interface Design Document (IDD)	The Interface Design Document contains the detailed design for the interface, including electrical characteristics, protocols, error correction schemes, data formats, and so on.
Version Description Document (VDD)	This document is basically a "packing list" of what is included in the release.
Software Test Plan (STP)	The Software Test Plan describes the software test environment, test resources required, and test schedule for one or more CSCIs.
Software Test Description (STD)	The Software Test Description contains the test cases and test procedures to be conducted for the CSCI.
Software Test Report (STR)	The Software Test Report describes the results of testing the CSCI.
Software User's Manual	The Software User's Manual describes how to operate the computer program.

IEEE

TABLE 5 DOCUMENTS INCLUDED IN IEEE STANDARD

Title	Description
Software Quality Assurance Plan (SQAP)	The Software Quality Assurance Plan covers management; documentation; standards, practices, conventions, and metrics; reviews and audits; tests; problem reporting and corrective action; tools, techniques, and methodologies; code control; media control; supplier control; records collection, maintenance, and retention; training; and risk management.
Software Configuration Management Plan (SCMP)	The Plan documents what configuration management activities are to be done, how they are to be done, who is responsible for doing specific activities, when they are to happen, and what resources are required.
Software Test Plan	This plan prescribes the scope, approach, resources, and schedule of the testing activities. It identifies the items being tested, the features to be tested, the testing tasks to be performed, the personnel responsible for each task, and the risks associated with this plan.

Title	Description
Test Design Specification	This document specifies refinements of the test approach and identifies the features to be tested by this design and its associated tests.
Test Case Specification	This document defines a test case identified by a test-design specification.
Test Procedure Specification	This document specifies the steps for executing a set of test cases or, more generally, the steps used to analyze a software item in order to evaluate a set of features.
Test Item Transmittal Report	This document identifies the test items being transmitted for testing. It includes the person responsible for each item, its physical location, and its status. Any variations from the current item requirements and designs are noted in this report.
Test Log	This document provides a chronological record of relevant details about the execution of tests.
Test Incident Report	This report documents any event that occurs during the testing process which requires investigation.
Test Summary Report	This document summarizes the results of the designated testing activities and provides evaluations based on these results.
Software Requirement Specification (SRS)	This document contains the essential requirements (functions, performance, design constraints, and attributes) of the software and its external interfaces.
Software Design Description	This document is a representation of software created to facilitate analysis, planning, implementation, and decision making. The Software Design Description is used as a medium for communicating software design information, and may be considered a blueprint or model of the system.
Software Project Management Plan	A Software Project Management Plan is the controlling document for managing a software project; it defines the technical and managerial processes necessary to satisfy the project requirements.
Software User's Manual	This document is the user documentation of program function.

MIL-STD-498

TABLE 6 DOCUMENTS INCLUDED IN MIL-STD-498

Title	Description
Software Development Plan (SDP)	The Software Development Plan (SDP) describes a developer's plans for conducting a software development effort. The term "software development" in this DID is meant to include new development, modification, reuse, reengineering, maintenance, and all other activities resulting in software products.
Software Installation Plan (SIP)	The Software Installation Plan (SIP) is a plan for installing software at user sites, including preparation, user training, and conversion from existing systems.
Software Transition Plan (STrP)	The Software Transition Plan (STrP) identifies the hardware, software, and other resources needed for life-cycle support of deliverable software and describes the developer's plans for transitioning deliverable items to the support agency.
Operational Concept Description (OCD)	The Operational Concept Description (OCD) describes a proposed system in terms of the user needs it will fulfill, its relationship to existing systems or procedures, and the ways it will be used.
System/Subsystem Specification (SSS)	The System/Subsystem Specification (SSS) specifies the requirements for a system or subsystem and the methods to be used to ensure that each requirement has been met. Requirements pertaining to the system's or subsystem's external interfaces may be presented in the SSS or in one or more Interface Requirements Specifications (IRSs) referenced from the SSS.
System/Subsystem Design Description (SSDD)	The System/Subsystem Design Description (SSDD) describes the system- or subsystem-wide design and its architectural design. The SSDD may be supplemented by Interface Design Descriptions (IDDs) and Database Design Descriptions (DBDDs).
Software Requirements Specification (SRS)	The Software Requirements Specification (SRS) specifies the requirements for a Computer Software Configuration Item (CSCI) and the methods to be used to ensure that each requirement has been met.

continued

Title	Description
	Requirements pertaining to the CSCI's external interfaces may be presented in the SRS or in one or more Interface Requirements Specifications (IRSs) referenced from the SRS.
Interface Requirements Specification (IRS)	The Interface Requirements Specification (IRS) specifies the requirements imposed on one or more systems, subsystems, Hardware Configuration Items (HWCIs), Computer Software Configuration Items (CSCIs), manual operations, or other system components to achieve one or more interfaces among these entities. An IRS can cover any number of interfaces.
Software Design Description (SDD)	The Software Design Description (SDD) describes the design of a Computer Software Configuration Item (CSCI). It describes the CSCI-wide design decisions, the CSCI architectural design, and the detailed design needed to implement the software. The SDD may be supplemented by Interface Design Descriptions (IDDs) and Database Design Descriptions (DBDDs).
Interface Design Description (IDD)	The Interface Design Description (IDD) describes the interface characteristics of one or more systems, subsystems, Hardware Configuration Items (HCWIs), Computer Software Configuration Items (CSCIs), manual operations, or other system components. An IDD may describe any number of interfaces.
Database Design Description (DBDD)	A Database Design Description (DBDD) describes the design of a database, that is, a collection of related data stored in one or more computerized files in a manner that can be accessed by users or computer programs via a database management system (DBMS). It can also describe the software units used to access or manipulate the data.
Software Test Plan (STP)	The Software Test Plan (STP) describes plans for qualification testing of Computer Software Configuration Items (CSCIs) and software systems. It describes the software test environment to be used for the testing, identifies the tests to be performed, and provides schedules for test activities.

continued

Title	Description
Software Test Description (STD)	The Software Test Description (STD) describes the test preparation, test cases, and test procedures to be used to perform qualification testing of a Computer Software Configuration Item (CSCI) or a software system or subsystem.
Software Test Report (STR)	The Software Test Report (STR) is a record of the qualification testing performed on a Computer Software Configuration Item (CSCI), a software system or subsystem, or other software related item.
Software Version Description (SVD)	The Software Version Description (SVD) identifies and describes a software version consisting of one or more Computer Software Configuration Items (CSCIs). It is used to release, track, and control software versions.
Software User Manual (SUM)	The Software User Manual (SUM) tells a hands-on software user how to install and use a Computer Software Configuration Item (CSCI), a group of related CSCIs, or a software system or subsystem. It may also cover a particular aspect of software operation, such as instructions for a particular position or task.
Software Center Operator Manual (SCOM)	The Software Center Operator Manual (SCOM) provides personnel in a computer center or other centralized or networked software installation with information on how to install and operate a software system.
Software Input/Output Manual (SIOM)	The Software Input/Output Manual (SIOM) tells a user how to access, submit inputs to, and interpret output from, a batch or interactive software system that is run by personnel in a computer center or other centralized or networked software installation.

Defining Your Own Software Development Standards

You can also define your own company specific standards. Quite often, the easiest approach to doing this is to select a pre-defined standard that is closest to the way you want to do business, then modify that. Rather than modifying the standard definition itself, however, it is better to make a copy of the standard with your own name, then modify that copy.

You can create your own tailored version of a standard in Cost•Xpert by pressing the **Amplify/Edit** button next to the"Standard"combo box.You can also select the menu choice **Maintain,** then **Standards.** The dialog shown in Figure 17 is then displayed.

Defining a standard involves the following steps:

1. Define the documents that make up the standard.
2. For each document, write up a description, then enter three coefficients.The coefficients are used when determining estimated page counts, and the coefficients define the page counts in the form of:

$$\text{Page Count} = A + (B * \text{Volume} ** C)$$

You will also normally want to create or modify a system life cycle that incorporates the documents you have defined for your standard. This process is covered below.

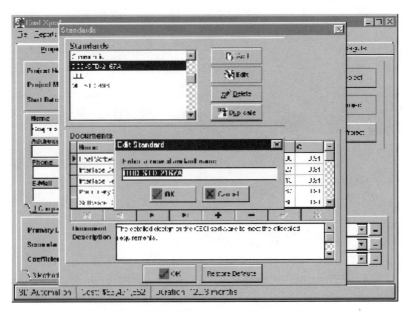

FIGURE 17 EDIT STANDARDS DIALOG BOX

SELECTING A PROJECT LIFE CYCLE

A project life cycle defines the activities that will be accomplished during the project. For each activity, the life cycle also includes the typical percentage of the total effort required for that activity and the project phase during which that activity is accomplished.

Cost•Xpert comes pre-initialized with the five most common life-cycle models:

TABLE 7 FIVE MOST COMMON LIFE CYCLE MODELS

Model	Description
Client-Server Medium	Medium sized (less than $1M) client-server development projects.
Client-Server Large	Large (over $1M) client-server development projects.
Standard—Small	Traditional development efforts that are under $100K in size.
Standard—Medium	Traditional development efforts that are between $100K and $1M in size.
Standard—Large	Traditional development efforts that are over $1M in size.

Defining Your Own Project Life Cycle

Figure 18 shows the pop-up form that can be used to see the specific tasks associated with each life-cycle model. Of course, you can also define your own models either from scratch or by copying and modifying one of the predefined models.

Defining Document Relationships

In addition to specifying the activities that make up a given life cycle, you must also map the documents required by each software development standard to the specific life-cycle phase where they are produced. Cost•Xpert comes pre-initialized with this information for all of the

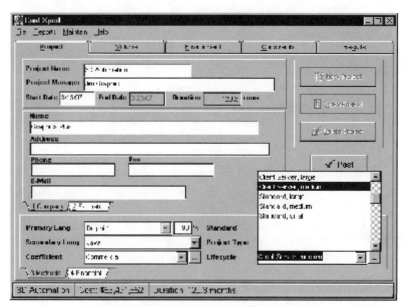

FIGURE 18 EDIT LIFE-CYCLE DIALOG BOX

available life cycles and standards. Once again, you can tailor this information. Figure 19 shows the form that would be used to perform this mapping. This form is accessed from the **Maintain** menu by selecting **Activity-Document Relationships.**

SELECTING A PROJECT TYPE

The Project Type determines the likely risk factors and projected defect rates and types. Cost•Xpert comes pre-initialized with the project types shown in Table 8.

As with other Cost•Xpert features, you can extend or modify the Cost•Xpert database by selecting **Maintain,** then **Project Types** from the main menu. The form shown in Figure 20 allows you to specify the most likely risk factors and defect percentages.

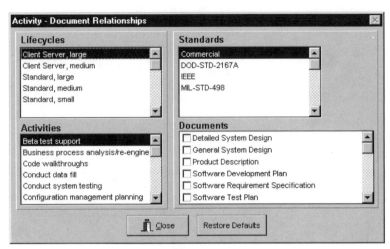

FIGURE 19 MAINTAIN ACTIVITY-DOCUMENT RELATIONSHIPS

TABLE 8 PROJECT TYPE

Project Type	Description
Commercial	Commercial development projects.
Embedded	Embedded programming (real time, embedded systems).
End User Computing	Development of applications by end users using high-level tools.
Military	Military development.
MIS	Management information systems development.
Outsourced	Projects that are outsourced to another company.
Systems	Systems projects, including operating systems, network operating systems, and telecommunications.

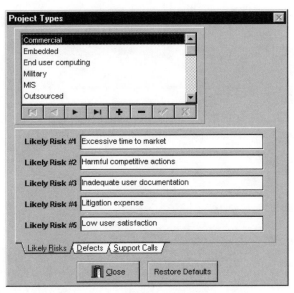

FIGURE 20 MAINTAIN PROJECT TYPES

ENTERING OTHER PROJECT FACTORS

The following additional factors should be entered on the project page, Financial Tab (Figure 21).

- Average Trip Cost—average cost for a trip between the development site and the customer site.
- Average Cost Per Hour—average cost per hour for the development team. Used to estimate total project cost.
- Inflation Factor—estimated inflation rate. Used for maintenance calculations.
- Number of Users—estimated number of users of the system.
- Annual Change Traffic—estimated percentage of the code that will change each year as a result of ongoing maintenance. This number typically varies between 3% and 20%, with 15% being the most likely percentage.

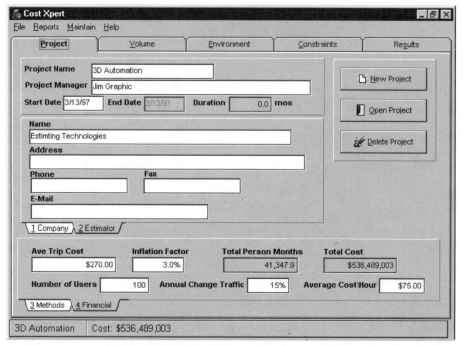

FIGURE 21 PROJECT SCREEN, FINANCIAL TAB

At this point, we've learned how to estimate the program's volume and how to specify high-level factors about the project that allow a generic estimate to be prepared. We haven't taken into account any of the project-specific factors yet. These factors include the capabilities of the staff and the stability of the requirements. This is the topic of our next chapter.

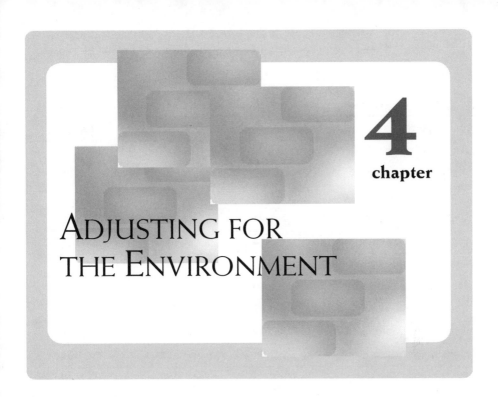

ADJUSTING FOR THE ENVIRONMENT

Obviously, the size of the development effort (the program volume) will have a significant impact on the project cost. In addition, your intuition must tell you that additional factors such as the experience and capabilities of the development team must also have a significant impact. In fact, the impact of factors such as these can often result in substantial variations in development efficiency and cost. Luckily, there is a quantitative, methodical approach to adjusting for these project-specific environmental factors.

VALUE OF ENVIRONMENTAL ADJUSTMENTS

Environmental factors can have a major influence over the development efficiency of your team. Factors are rated using a scale of Very Low, Low, Normal, High, or Very High using specific guidelines covered later in this chapter. A value of 1.0 for an environmental factor means that the default equations should apply. A value of 1.5 means that the default calculated cost would be increased by 50%. A value of 0.5 means that the default calculated cost would be decreased by 50%. Table 9 provides you with a rough idea of the magnitude of impact you may observe from some of the various environmental factors.

TABLE 9 IMPACT FROM ENVIRONMENTAL FACTORS

Factor	Very low	Normal	Very high
Analyst capability	1.46	1.00	0.71
Programmer capability	1.42	1.00	0.70
Applications experience	1.29	1.00	0.82
Virtual machine experience	1.21	1.00	0.90
Prog. language experience	1.14	1.00	0.95
Execution time constraint	1.00	1.00	1.30
Main storage constraint	1.00	1.00	1.21
Virtual machine volatility	0.87	1.00	1.30
Computer turnaround time	0.79	1.00	1.15
Requirements volatility	0.91	1.00	1.38
Product reliability	0.75	1.00	1.40
Database size	0.94	1.00	1.16
Product complexity	0.70	1.00	1.30
Required reuse	1.00	1.00	1.30
Modern programming pract.	1.24	1.00	0.82
Use of S/W tools	1.24	1.00	0.83

The numbers in the above table were empirically determined from extensive work by Barry Boehm, Capers Jones, and others. They have been validated against over 2,000 projects.

General Approach to Adjusting for the Environment

For each factor, the analyst assigns a value of Very Low, Low, Normal, High, or Very High. A description appropriate for each rating is standardized to keep the ratings as objective as possible. In Cost•Xpert, these values are entered on the Environment tab (see Figure 22). The factors can be broken down in the general categories of team experience; project

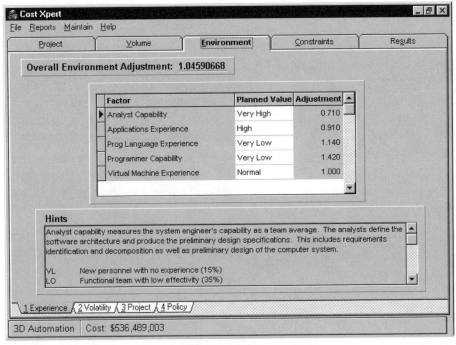

FIGURE 22 ENVIRONMENT TAB

volatility; project characteristics; and management policy. Each of these categories will be addressed individually.

Additional Uses of the Information

The obvious value of these environmental factors, and their primary use, is to allow you to better estimate the costs for a specific software project. Many managers find that this information has a significant additional value when doing a cost-benefit analysis.

If you scan the table of environmental factors, you will see that many of them are under your control. Obvious examples include the use of modern programming practices and the use of software tools. For a specific development team, even less obvious factors such as the average experience of your development team may also be under your control.

You can normally quantify the cost of improving your "score" in these areas. The difficult part is quantifying the benefit to be gained by this expenditure of organizational resources. These environmental factor values provide you with exactly this information. For example, you can use Cost•Xpert to determine the exact value of moving your organization from Normal to High with respect to the use of modern programming practices. If you multiply this delta by the total software development budget impacted by the change, you can determine the specific financial benefit to be gained.

In the remainder of this chapter, we provide you with the specific guidelines used when setting the various factors. This information is also available on-line in Cost•Xpert.

TEAM EXPERIENCE ADJUSTMENTS

Analyst Capability

Analyst capability measures the system engineers' capability as a team average. The analysts define the software architecture and produce the preliminary design specifications. This includes working on the requirements identification and decomposition, as well as creating a preliminary design of the computer system.

VL   New personnel with no experience (15%)
LO   Functional team with low effectiveness (35%)
NM   Average team with nominal effectiveness (55%)
HI   Strong team with good effectiveness (75%)
VH   Strong team with many top people (90%)

Project Application Experience

Project application experience measures the familiarity of the design and development team with this specific application area.

VL   Less than 1 year
LO   Less than 3 years
NM   Less than 6 years

| HI | Less than 12 years |
| VH | Over 12 years |

Language Experience

Language experience measures the design and programming team's experience with the programming language, which will be used to implement the design in the software.

VL	Never used before
LO	Less than 1 year experience
NM	At least 1 year experience
HI	2 years experience
VH	More than 2 years experience

Programming Team Capability

Programming team capability measures the capability of the programmers who will actually perform the detailed design and write/test the physical code during the coding and unit testing phases.

VL	15th percentile team
LO	35th percentile team
NM	55th percentile team
HI	75th percentile team
VH	90th percentile team

Virtual Machine Experience

Virtual machine experience measures the design and programming team's experience with the virtual machine. The virtual machine includes the actual target physical hardware, operating system, development environment, database management system, and similar environmental tools.

VL	Never used before
LO	Less than 6 months of experience
NM	Less than 1 year of experience

HI   Less than 2 years of experience
VH   More than 2 years of experience

PROJECT VOLATILITY ADJUSTMENTS

Requirement Volatility

Requirement volatility measures the amount of project design and development rework that results from changes in customer specified requirements. This factor can have a very large effect on the total development effort, but should be used very carefully. Most projects will be put on a contract after negotiations based on the known requirements. The expectation is that any changes in the requirements will result in an engineering change proposal that will adjust the contract price accordingly. This factor compensates for the extra system engineering and management effort required to evaluate the changes in requirements, estimate the design impacts, prepare the engineering change proposals, and change the software.

VL   Essentially none
LO   Small, non-critical redirections
NM   Occasional moderate redirections
HI   Frequent moderate or occasional major redirections
VH   Frequent major redirections

Virtual Machine Volatility

Virtual machine volatility measures the amount of changes that the virtual machine is expected to need during the design and development phases. The virtual machine includes the actual target physical hardware, operating system, development environment, database management system, and similar environmental tools.

VL   No changes expected
LO   One change every 6 months
NM   One change every 3 months
HI   One change every month
VH   Several changes every month

PROJECT CHARACTERISTIC ADJUSTMENTS

Computer Turnaround Time

Computer turnaround time measures the time spent waiting for the development environment to complete the compilation and for the modified code to be ready for testing. If testing requires that the compiled code be downloaded to a target computer, this download time must be included.

VL Less than 6 minutes
LO Less than 30 minutes
NM Less than 4 hours
HI Less than 12 hours
VH More than 12 hours

Database Size

Data base size determines the effects on the software development due to the size of the database that must be maintained and manipulated. D/P is the database size (bytes) divided by the program size (lines of code).

VL Very small effort (D/P < 10)
LO Very small effort (D/P < 10)
NM Nominal size effort (10 <= D/P < 100)
HI Large and complex effort (100 <= D/P < 1000)
VH Very large and complicated effort (D/P >= 1000)

Execution Time Constraints

Execution time constraints measures the approximate percentage of the available CPU execution time that will be used by the software in order to achieve the system's performance objectives.

VL No constraints on execution time
LO No constraints on execution time
NM 60% utilization

HI   85% utilization
VH   95% utilization

Main Storage Constraints

Main storage constraints measures the amount of constraint imposed on the software due to main memory limitations in the target computer. If memory is a problem, more time must be spent on design and coding.

VL   No memory constraints
LO   No memory constraints
NM   No memory constraints
HI   70% utilization
VH   85% utilization

Software Product Complexity

Software product complexity quantifies the complexity of the software product that is to be developed.

VL   Off-line simple print routines
LO   Off-line batch processes
NM   Data processing, some business math
HI   Some hardware I/O or advanced data structures
VH   Real time, advanced math, very complex

Required Software Reliability

Required software reliability quantifies the required reliability of the finished software. As the required reliability increases, more time must be spent in the critical design and testing phases. The values describe the impact on the user of a software failure.

VL   Slight inconvenience
LO   Easily recoverable loss
NM   Moderate recoverable loss
HI   MIL-STD or high financial loss
VH   Possible loss of life

MANAGEMENT POLICY ADJUSTMENTS

Modern Programming Practices

Modern programming practices quantifies the use of modern programming practices such as structured design, object-oriented design, formal data design methodologies, etc.

VL   No use
LO   Beginning use
NM   Some use by experienced team members
HI   General use by all team members
VH   Routine use with strong company training

Required Reusability

Required reusability measures the extra effort needed to generalize software modules when they must be developed specifically for reuse in other software programs.

VL   Not for reuse elsewhere
LO   Not for reuse elsewhere
NM   Not for reuse elsewhere
HI   Reuse within a single application area
VH   Reuse across product line

Classified Application

Classified application measures the extra work required to develop software either in a classified security area or for a classified security application.

VL   Unclassified
LO   Unclassified
NM   Unclassified
HI   Classified
VH   Classified

Software Tools

Software tools measures the use of automated software tools such as computer aided software engineering (CASE), an Ada programming support environment, integrated team development and test environments, and so on.

VL   Very few, primitive tools
LO   Good compilers, few support tools
NM   Good core tools
HI   Extensive tools, but not well integrated
VH   Fully integrated development environment

So far, we have described how to define the project volume, how to specify project characteristics such as the development life cycle, and how to adjust for the project development environment. The result will be an estimated software cost and an optimal project schedule. Quite often, however, you may be asked to adjust the schedule either to deliver the completed code at an accelerated pace, or to stretch the schedule out to improve efficiency. Any adjustment to the schedule will have a cost impact, and the approach to quantifying that impact is the subject of our next chapter.

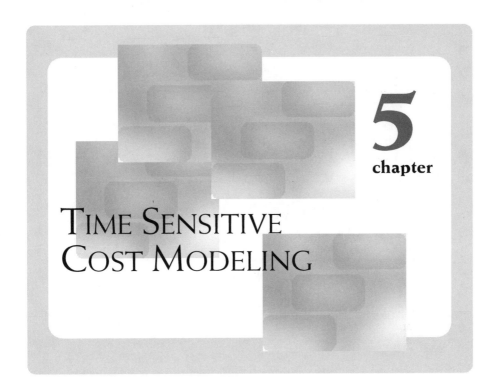

5
chapter

TIME SENSITIVE COST MODELING

The coefficients that you use to estimate the total software cost also dictate the optimal project schedule. In this chapter, we'll look at how that optimal project schedule is derived, and also look at the quantitative cost impact of other schedules.

OPTIMAL PROJECT STAFFING CURVES

Norden discovered that optimal project staffing for typical projects that require communication and learning follows a Rayleigh distribution. This curve ramps up relatively steeply, then trails off gradually, resulting in a rough wave shape. Putnam confirmed that this result applied to software development projects. Figure 23 shows the optimal staffing curve for a hypothetical project. This characteristic curve is known as the Putnam-Norden-Rayleigh (PNR) staffing curve.

Of course, the PNR model covers the entire life cycle from development through maintenance. The portion of the curve from initiation through peak staffing corresponds to the staffing curve during development; the portion of the curve from this peak through the gradual taper-

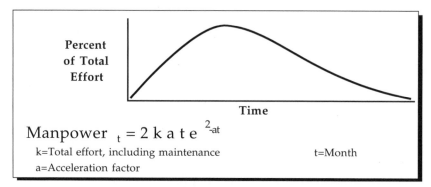

$$\text{Manpower}_t = 2kate^{-at^2}$$

k=Total effort, including maintenance   t=Month

a=Acceleration factor

FIGURE 23 PNR STAFFING CURVE

off defines the requirements for pilot testing, rollout, and maintenance (Figure 24).

Although the curves are common sense, it is amazing to realize how many projects run into difficulties by attempting to use a staffing profile that is roughly flat. This results in a situation where the early part of the project has too many developers and a significant amount of resultant inefficiency, while the peak part of the project (near the scheduled completion date) is understaffed. This situation is shown in Figure 25.

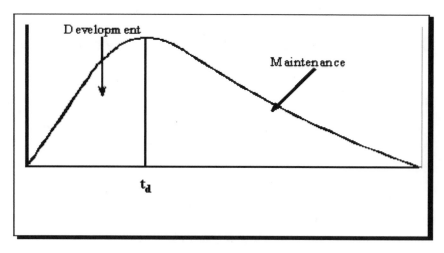

FIGURE 24 PNR LIFE CYCLE MODEL

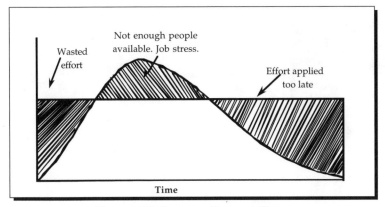

FIGURE 25 STAFFING PROFILE CURVE

THE TIME/COST TRADE-OFF

All of the costing formulas used in this book start by assuming that the project is developed over the optimal period of time. Optimal development time, or T_d, is the development time that is optimal in terms of both the development schedule and required resources. However, there are a variety of reasons you might want to develop your project using a different schedule. As shown in Figure 26, you can reduce your costs by increasing your development time up to T_o, which is defined as the optimal development time in terms of cost. T_o has been empirically determined to be twice T_d and to result in a cost reduction by 50%. As you increase the cost beyond T_o, the costs begin to climb again at a roughly linear rate.

Although it is unusual for a project schedule to be pushed beyond T_d, it is common for software to be required prior to the time allowed by T_d. Accelerating the development schedule is possible, but the cost penalties are severe. As shown in Figure 26, the costs climb exponentially as the project schedule is accelerated.

AVOIDING THE IMPOSSIBLE REGION

In a study of over 750 projects which attempted to deliver the code in less than T_d, none of the projects successfully achieved a crashed schedule

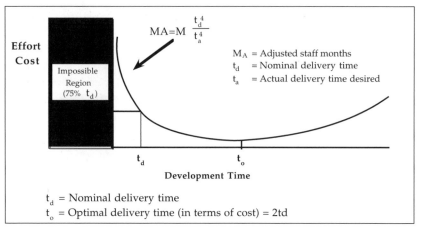

FIGURE 26 REDUCE COSTS, INCREASE DEVELOPMENT TIME

beyond 75% T_d. Researchers noted this phenomena and this barrier has become known as the *impossible region,* because it is impossible to accelerate the schedule beyond this amount using traditional development approaches.

As shown in Figure 27, Cost•Xpert allows you to adjust the project schedule in the range between the impossible region and T_o while adjusting the cost accordingly. The default schedule is T_d.

ALTERNATE STRATEGIES FOR ACCELERATING DELIVERY

There are times when you simply must accelerate the schedule beyond that allowed by the impossible region. When faced with this requirement, there are four basic approaches that you can follow:

1. Reduce functionality,
2. Decouple tasks,
3. Use redundant parallel development, and
4. Increase reuse.

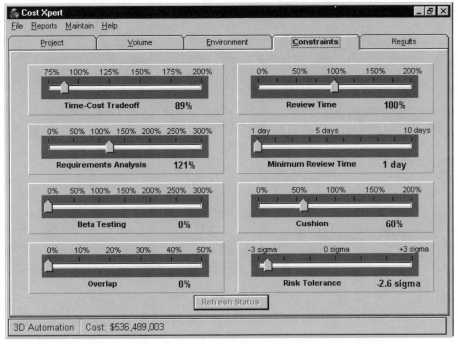

FIGURE 27 CONSTRAINTS SCREEN, TIME/COST TRADE-OFF

Reduce Functionality

The best approach is to reduce functionality. In other words, scale back the volume to be created (functionality) to reduce both the cost and the required schedule.

Decouple Tasks

The cost schedule curves are based on a single project with complex interactions. If you decouple, you can increase parallelism and reduce both schedule and cost. For example, if you can split one project into two that have minimal and well-defined interactions, then both projects can be costed and scheduled independently. This is the real power of object-oriented development (e.g., C++, Object Pascal).

Use Redundant Parallel Development

True redundant parallel development can significantly decrease your schedule if you have the resources (people and money) available. Basically, you assign multiple teams to write the same component. The first team to finish has their code used. The other code is either discarded or used as a back-up in case of inefficiencies or bugs with the winner's code. This can be repeated for each program module.

Increase Reuse

Increasing reuse can significantly lower your development schedule. This is the true power of component-based development environments such as Delphi and Visual Basic.

OTHER FACTORS INFLUENCING PROJECT SCHEDULE AND COST

There are other factors that influence both the project's schedule and cost. These are controlled by the project estimator/manager in Cost•Xpert using the other controls available on the Constraints tab. Each will be addressed below.

Requirements Analysis Time

The time spent on requirements analysis will vary significantly from project to project. If you are a contractor and the requirements are provided to you by the customer, you may spend zero time on requirements analysis. On the other hand, if you are beginning a complex project with very uncertain requirements, you may spend considerable effort in requirements analysis activities. Cost•Xpert uses standard numbers for requirements analysis effort, but allows you to adjust the time from 0% (none) to 300% (three times the standard amount of effort spent on requirements analysis). Because some form of requirements understanding is needed for all jobs, you may still see requirement related tasks on the recommended task list; but the effort will be proportionately reduced.

Beta Testing Time

Beta testing is the system testing after development and prior to final roll-out. In commercial environments, it is sometimes known as pilot testing. For military projects, it is sometimes known as operational testing. Once again, the time spent on this activity for a given project can vary from 0% to 300%. Because some form of final testing is needed for all jobs, you may still see beta testing tasks on the recommended task list; but the effort will be proportionately reduced.

Task Overlap

By default, Cost•Xpert assumes that tasks that are dependent on each other are executed sequentially. In other words, if Task A is dependent on Task B, then Task B cannot start until Task A is complete. You can reduce the schedule (and increase the cost) by increasing the degree of task overlap from 0% through 50%.

Review Time

Cost•Xpert allows time for customers to review the various specifications and other deliverables that are produced. You can reduce both cost and time if you are confident that the customer can turn around those review documents faster (0% implies a same day response). Similarly, you can increase both the schedule and the cost if the customer is expected to be slower in reviewing the documents.

Minimum Review Time

Cost•Xpert assumes that in an emergency, you can answer a customer's key technical question in one day. If the customer has a longer turn-around than one day, then both the schedule and the cost will increase. You can adjust the minimum review time from 1 day through 10 days based on the customer with whom you are working.

The remaining two control sliders on the Constraint tab allow you to adjust the project schedule and cost based on your risk tolerance, which is the topic of our next chapter.

RISK AND SENSITIVITY ANALYSIS

6

A key aspect of software cost and schedule estimating is performing a risk and sensitivity analysis. The risk analysis quantifies the project risk and adjusts the cost and schedule based on your risk tolerance. The sensitivity analysis identifies factors that adversely impact your planned costs and that must be carefully managed.

ADJUSTING THE CUSHION

The simplest form of risk management is to simply add a fixed percentage to the calculated cost to use as contingency funds. This cushion (sort of a management slush fund) does not impact the schedule, but is available to assist management in overcoming problems. The default of Cost•Xpert is 0%, (no contingency funds). It is not unusual for contractors to vary the amount of contingency funds based on the nature of the contract. For example, contractors may add 40% contingency funds to fixed-price contracts. This adjustment can also be used to compensate for customers who are known to be difficult to please. In Cost•Xpert, the adjustment is made using the Cushion slider on the Constraints tab.

67

ADJUSTING RISK TOLERANCE

Cost•Xpert calculates the mean schedule and cost based on all of the input parameters. Because this number is the mean, it implies that half the jobs will exceed this amount and half will not reach this amount. This is the correct definition of an estimate, but some situations require that you diverge from this number.

The amount of spread in your estimate is measured in terms of the standard deviation. At a +3 standard deviation, you can be 99% confident that the project will come in under your estimate in terms of schedule and cost. At a –3 standard deviation, you will come in under budget and under schedule only 1% of the time. Cost•Xpert allows you to set your risk tolerance between a –3 standard deviation and +3 standard deviation. You might set the number below 0 if the project is strategically important and you are willing to risk the probability that you will overrun. You might set the number above 0 if the consequences of being over budget or late are especially severe.

You can also turn to the Results tab, Risk sub-tab in Cost•Xpert and review the risk tolerance comparisons directly. This grid shows you the estimated cost and schedule at whole number increments from a –3 standard deviation to a +3 standard deviation (Figure 28).

LIKELY RISK FACTORS

On the same sub-tab, Cost•Xpert identifies the most likely risk factors for this project. You can review this list to determine those factors that you feel apply to this project. Those should be checked so that they will print out on a risk report. You can also add new risk factors from this sub-tab.

PERFORMING A SENSITIVITY ANALYSIS

Your estimated costs will vary based on the environmental factors that you entered. There is a risk that your assumptions in this area might be incorrect because of changes made prior to the project or during the project. For example, suppose that you assumed that an experienced team would be doing the development work. You set the environmental factors

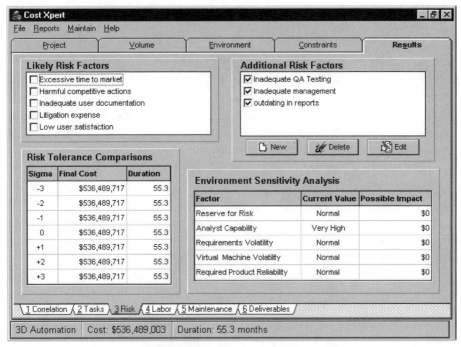

FIGURE 28 RESULTS TAB, RISK SUB-TAB

accordingly. Now suppose management decides to use that team on a different project and provides you with a team of new college graduates. Some of the fundamental environmental factors you entered are now totally incorrect and the cost estimate is equally flawed.

Cost•Xpert automatically scans the environmental factors that you entered and looks for those where a small change would have a major negative impact on the project's total cost. It displays the main factors and the possible impact if the factor varied by one level (to look at the impact of changes of more than one level, you need to manually change the value and record the cost difference). These are factors that you should watch closely during development. In addition, in the written report documenting your cost estimate, you should stress that the costs are contingent on these environmental values not changing. If management does insist on removing that team of experienced programmers, you should immediately quantify the cost impact and ensure that everyone involved understands exactly how much that action will cost the project.

FEEDING DATA TO RISK•XPERT

Risk•Xpert is a tool that supports both risk assessment and contingency planning and tracking to mitigate risks in a formal, optimized manner. Cost•Xpert can feed project related risk factors directly into Risk•Xpert to serve as a starting point in your risk management activities. For more information on Risk•Xpert, contact *info@marotz.com* or visit *www.marotz.com*.

In addition to the risk information, Cost•Xpert provides a wealth of additional information about the project based on your inputs. This information is the subject of our next chapter.

ADDITIONAL COST•XPERT OUTPUTS

The core of any cost estimating system is a bottom line cost for the project, normally supplemented with a schedule. In addition, however, there is a wealth of other information that can be gleaned from the extensive databases of projects that went into Cost•Xpert. These additional outputs are the subject of this chapter.

COST ALLOCATIONS AND TASK LISTS

Preparing a cost and schedule estimate for a project has two distinct parts: estimating and allocation. *Estimating* involves determining the total cost and time required to complete the project. It is a single lump sum amount of time and money. *Allocating* involves taking that time and money and apportioning it among the phases, people, and tasks.

The first step in the allocation process is to determine the tasks that need to be accomplished, the phases of development where those tasks will be completed, and the optimal staffing mixture for each phase. This is defined when you select a project life cycle. The life cycle determines the tasks that must be performed and the percentage of the total effort each task will require. In addition, the tasks are assigned to project phases to allow Cost•Xpert to predict the optimal labor mix for each task.

The final recommended tasks are shown on the Tasks sub-tab of the Results notebook tab in Cost•Xpert (Figure 29). Along with the tasks, the tool identifies the deliverables that should be produced, the percent of total effort allocated to that task, the cost for that task, and the recommended task duration. This information can then form the basis of a project plan, which may be tracked using standard project management software.

LABOR LOADING BY PHASE AND CATEGORY

Cost•Xpert determines the optimal staff levels, by labor category, for each month of the project. This information is displayed on the Labor sub-tab of the Results notebook tab in Cost•Xpert (Figure 30). The graph

Task ID	Task	Deliverable	% of Total	Cost	Duration
1	Code Modules		0.25%	$1,341,222	0.0
1.1	New				
1.2	Graphics Library				
1.3	Rectangle Lib				
2	Activities				
2.1	Project planning		1.00%	$5,364,890	0.0
2.1.1	Perform Activity				
2.2	Configuration management planning		0.25%	$1,341,222	0.0
2.2.1	Perform Activity				
2.3	Quality assurance planning		0.50%	$2,682,445	0.0
2.3.1	Perform Activity				
2.4	Status reporting		4.00%	$21,459,560	0.0
2.4.1	Perform Activity				

Total $536,489,003

1 Correlation / 2 Tasks / 3 Risk / 4 Labor / 5 Maintenance / 6 Deliverables

3D Automation   Cost: $536,489,003

FIGURE 29 RESULTS SCREEN, TASKS SUB-TAB

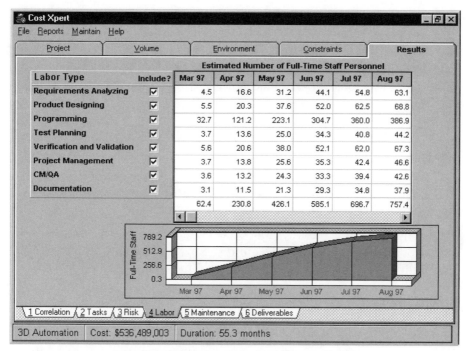

FIGURE 30 RESULTS SCREEN, LABOR SUB-TAB

at the bottom of the form shows the total labor level by month for all of the checked labor categories.

MAINTENANCE AND LIFE-CYCLE COSTS

Cost•Xpert provides three life-cycle cost outputs: maintenance, defects, and support calls.

Software Maintenance Estimates

Software maintenance includes software repairs and software updates, but does not include major rewrites of the software that substantially change the functionality of the available software.

This should normally be treated as a separate, follow-on project. Maintenance can be categorized at a high level into:

- Corrective maintenance—Correcting software defects (bugs).
- Adaptive maintenance—Adapting the software to handle changes in the environment, including things like changes to the operating system, database management system, and input files.
- Perfective maintenance—Making improvements in the software's functionality, usability, reliability, performance, or security.

Figure 31 shows the U.S. average distribution of maintenance activities broken down by category.

The actual maintenance efforts predicted by Cost•Xpert have been proven to closely match actual, observed maintenance costs as shown in Figure 32.

Using this information, Cost•Xpert predicts both the maintenance effort for each year of the project and the projected maintenance, adjusted for inflation (Figure 33).

Software Defect Estimates

The second output available on the same screen is the estimated defects by year, along with a breakdown showing the estimated defects by defect

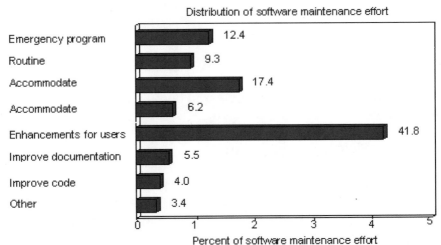

FIGURE 31 MAINTENANCE ACTIVITIES BROKEN DOWN BY CATEGORY

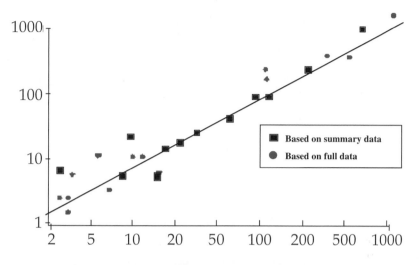

FIGURE 32 ACTUAL, OBSERVED MAINTENANCE COSTS

Cost Xpert				_ 🗗 ✕

File Reports Maintain Help

Project	Volume	Environment	Constraints	**Results**

Number of Users: 100   **Annual Change Traffic: 15%**

Year	Labor (Number of Staff)	Cost	Defects	Support Calls
1	775.3	$124,331,323	**248,087** Requirement: 14,885 Design: 2,481 Coding: 2,481 Docs: 2,481 Bad Fixes:2,481	155
2	671.9	$110,986,424	**206,740** Requirement: 12,404 Design: 2,067 Coding: 2,067 Docs: 2,067 Bad Fixes:2,067	55
3	594.4	$101,125,705	**82,696** Requirement: 4,962 Design: 827 Coding: 827 Docs: 827 Bad Fixes:827	55
4	516.8	$90,573,455	**82,696** Requirement: 4,962 Design: 827 Coding: 827 Docs: 827 Bad Fixes:827	55

\ 1 Correlation / 2 Tasks / 3 Risk / 4 Labor \ 5 Maintenance / 6 Deliverables /

3D Automation   Cost: $536,489,003

FIGURE 33 RESULTS SCREEN, MAINTENANCE SUB-TAB

category. This information is useful when planning your maintenance effort, but is even more useful when assessing system quality. If the system has significantly more defects than predicted by the industry averages shown in Cost•Xpert, then you might want to look at your software process and your quality assurance activities. If the system has significantly less defects than predicted by the industry averages, then you might want to reward the team and look for techniques that can be applied to other projects.

Support Calls

Finally, Cost•Xpert predicts the number of support calls that you will receive in each year following the introduction of the software. The call volume will tend to peak during times when you release new versions of the software.

DELIVERABLE ESTIMATES

The final sub-tab on the Cost•Xpert Results notebook tab is entitled Deliverables (Figure 34). This sub-tab lists the deliverables that should be produced (based on the software development standard that you are using); provides you with a description of each deliverable; and provides you with an estimated page count.

The page count is useful for two reasons. First, if the delivered document deviates significantly from the estimated page count, you might question whether the document is sufficient. Although this is not always a problem, you may be concerned when the prediction calls for a 1,000-page document and you're handed a 20-page pamphlet! Second, the numbers are useful when you're required to review the documents as they are produced and you would like to estimate the magnitude of the work that will be required.

Some additional documentation-related metrics are sometimes useful.

Capers Jones has determined that on the average, companies spend between two and four hours per page for technical documents. We have used 1.75 hours per page (one round of revisions only) with good luck, assuming that the conceptual work was already complete.

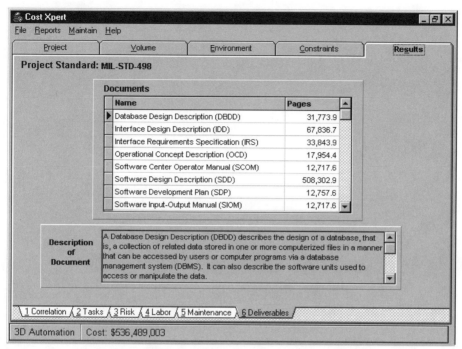

FIGURE 34 RESULTS SCREEN, MAINTENANCE SUB-TAB

While tracking the time required to write user's manuals and produce on-line help systems, we have found that it takes 1.5 hours per page for user's manuals (includes screen shots and assumes that you use some boilerplate formats), and that it takes an additional one hour per page to convert the document into a decent on-line help file. This does not include time spent doing exceptionally fancy tasks like creating hot spots embedded in complex graphics.

These examples show how tracking metrics regarding productivity can help you when preparing effective estimates. If you build a lot of software, you can collect sufficient metric information to precisely tailor estimating coefficients to your particular organization. This is the topic of the next chapter.

GATHERING METRICS, TAILORING COEFFICIENTS

8

chapter

As delivered, Cost•Xpert is tailored for an average project in an average organization. You already know how to use various factors, including the environmental factors, to tailor Cost•Xpert to your particular project. Unfortunately, your organization itself may not be typical. The result will be cost and schedule estimates that are consistently too high or too low. To tailor Cost•Xpert to your organization, you must gather some metric information and tailor the Cost•Xpert coefficients. This is the topic of this chapter.

TAILORING COST•XPERT CURVES

The core costing equations of Cost•Xpert involve a relatively simple equation of the form:

$$\boxed{\text{Effort} = a * \text{volume } \beta}$$

α and β are the organization specific coefficients that we use when describing the process of tailoring the coefficients. Let's look at the impact of these two coefficients on the costing curves, and how you might tailor them.

Modifying Alpha

As shown in Figure 35, we can explore the impact of modifying alpha alone by setting beta to 1.0. With an alpha of 1.0, the line moves up at a diagonal. This would say that for every increase in program volume, we have an exactly equal increase in program cost. As alpha becomes larger than 1.0, the slope of the line increases, but it remains linear. In other words, the cost per unit of volume has gone up, but the cost remains directly proportional to the volume. Similarly, as alpha goes below 1.0, the slope of the line decreases. The cost remains linear, but the cost per unit of volume is decreased. Alpha is primarily related to the efficiency of your development environment.

Modifying Beta

In Figure 36, alpha is set to 1.0 and we explore the effect of modifying beta. Because alpha is constant at 1.0, it has no impact on the resultant curves. If we set beta to 1.0, then the result is a straight line along the diagonal. Once again, the efficiency of our development (in terms of cost

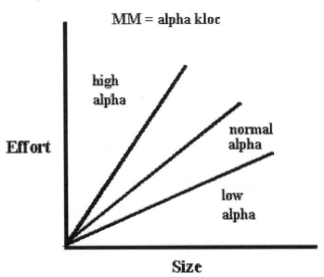

FIGURE 35 MODIFYING ALPHA

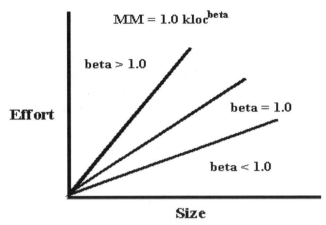

$$MM = 1.0 \, kloc^{beta}$$

beta > 1.0

beta = 1.0

beta < 1.0

Effort

Size

FIGURE 36 MODIFYING BETA

per volume delivered) does not change with project size. If beta is greater than 1.0, then the curve slopes upward. This means that as the projects get larger, the cost per unit of volume produced goes up. If beta is less than 1.0, then the curve slopes downward. This means that as the projects get larger, the cost per unit of volume produced goes down. For most projects, beta should be larger than 1.0 because communication difficulties tend to reduce efficiency as the project size increases. In fact, the only recorded case where beta is less than 1.0 is in the case of Ada development for military projects. There is speculation that this is caused by the steep learning curve for Ada, especially in a military project, and the fact that larger projects gain the advantage of better absorbing this learning curve and improving reuse of Ada code within the project framework.

The factors that impact beta are the efficiency of communication within your organization, and how effectively you are able to decouple the project tasks from each other. An example of a technology designed to help you decouple tasks is object-oriented development.

GATHERING METRICS

The minimum metrics that you will want to capture are the actual values for each of the raw inputs to CostüXpert. This should include the appropriate volume data (lines-of-code, function points, GUI metrics, and object metrics), the actual environmental factors, and the observed project behavior with respect to each of the project constraints.

If you are establishing a new metric program, you may want to add some additional information that is helpful, but not required.

This may include:

- Defect rates and severity,
- User satisfaction scores,
- Staffing information, divided by activity and phase,
- Deliverables information (title, page count, cost, and effort).

When you are gathering your metric data, you will want to capture the estimating data at the project start. You should then collect time, cost, and defect related data during the project.

TAILORING THE COEFFICIENTS

The first step in tailoring the coefficients is to use the actual values for a given project to perform an estimate. Enter the actual volume data, the actual observed values for the environmental factors, and the actual values for each of the project constraints. For discretionary constraints such as cushion and risk tolerance, set the value to the default. Look at the cost estimate predicted by Cost•Xpert and compare it to the actual, observed costs.

If the costs are consistently too low, then you need to increase alpha. If the costs are consistently too high, then you need to decrease alpha. This adjustment can be made as soon as you have completed your first one or two projects.

This form of adjustment will work if all projects are of a similar size to the ones used during the tailoring, or if your organization's efficiency varies with project size in accordance with industry norms.

After you have gathered metric data for several projects, including projects of varying size, you can tailor the project to your organization by fitting a curve with the appropriate equation to the observed data. This can be accomplished by someone on your staff or someone from a local university with a math background.

The information covered in this book is geared toward predicting software costs. In the next chapter, we look at some techniques you can use to improve your organization's software productivity and thus reduce software costs.

9
chapter

REDUCING COSTS

This chapter focuses on strategies you can employ to improve the efficiency of your development efforts and thereby reduce your costs. In terms of cost coefficients, we are looking at ways to both improve our environmental factors and to reduce our alpha coefficient.

COST REDUCTION, THE BIG PICTURE

Although this chapter focuses on reducing development costs, it is important to see this in light of the big picture. Enterprise costs (operational impact of the underlying information technology) are by far the biggest factor in terms of overall costs and in terms of impact on the success of the organization. This says that the most important consideration is to ensure that you are building the correct software in the first place. Here we are focused on effectiveness. It is far better for an organization to be effective but not efficient rather than be efficient but not effective.

Life-cycle costs (maintenance, training, support, and deployment) are typically much larger than the development costs. This justifies spending more up-front if it will significantly reduce ongoing maintenance and support costs. This is the area where object-oriented development tends to be strongest. Here we have a balance between effectiveness and efficiency.

Finally, there are the development costs. Here, we are focused on efficiency. Unfortunately, this is the primary focus of most cost reduction strategies even though it is the smallest cost driver! There is not enough material available for us to discuss reducing life-cycle costs effectively, and reducing enterprise costs is the topic of our strategic planning tool, Strategy•Xpert.

FOUR BASIC COST REDUCTION STRATEGIES

To reduce project costs, there are four primary alternatives:

1. You can reduce developed functionality by reducing delivered functionality, or by increasing reuse. This will reduce program volume.
2. We've seen that increasing the schedule to T_o, or twice T_d, will reduce costs by approximately one-half.
3. Environmental factors will often have a tremendous impact on cost. For example, bringing in a very strong development team will often reduce costs by over 50%.
4. Finally, you can adjust the curve coefficients by changing the development environment within your organization.

But before we cover these rather conventional techniques, let's explore some popular silver bullets that are advertised to do the equivalent of helping you "lose 30 pounds in 30 days while growing a new, full head of hair."

SOME SILVER BULLETS

Computer Aided Software Engineering (CASE) Tools

Computer Assisted Software Engineering (CASE), has been advertised as providing productivity gains of 100% to 1000%. Let's look at the reality.

- There is typically a 12- to 18-month enterprise learning curve prior to any productivity gain.
- Productivity gains of 5% to 10% are typical.
- CASE tools are the largest contributor, in terms of dollars, to corporate shelfware.

Let's look at some specific problems with CASE tools.

- Leaping into a new technology before you look into the methodology itself (do not touch that tool until you know your methodology).

  CASE tools are power tools to implement one or more development methodologies. If you can't effectively do the methodology using pen and paper, the CASE tool will just help you produce a lot of garbage very quickly.

- This may be the straw that broke the camel's back.

  CASE tools actually reduce productivity for the first 12 to 18 months. They are typically introduced only when the developers are totally swamped. The additional learning curve and productivity decrease may not be supportable.

- Many people underestimate planning and training requirements.

  CASE sales representatives seldom stress adequate training because it makes the sale more difficult and they often get no commission on training. The training costs are likely to be far more than the tool costs.

- The tool may not work as advertised.

  One programmer created a sign, "The XYZ CASE tool has thousands of features, hundreds of which are documented and dozens of which work."

- There is the issue of unpaid overtime.

  If the efficiency improvements result in shorter work weeks, but you weren't paying for the long weeks, then the true savings are zero.

Fourth Generation Languages

Fourth generation languages (e.g., database languages) have been tout-
ed as silver bullets that will solve the world's development problems.
Table 10 shows the kinds of results that are possible using fourth generation languages on small projects. In this case, Cobol and a popular 4GL
were used to deliver a small application with identical functionality.

TABLE 10 POSSIBLE 4GL RESULTS

Measure	Cobol	4GL
Lines-of-code	1,000	50
Schedule	2.8	0.3
Development effort	3.0	0.4
Cost	$16.5K	$2K

But there are problems with 4GLs. For example:

- They typically only work within limited problem domains.
- They are often not scalable.

Here's a true example.

A motor vehicle department wanted to implement a new system.
They did a pilot system using a 4GL and loved it. They tried it in a field
office and it was great. They developed the entire system and came in
under budget and on time. They deployed it statewide and found that
the response time was approximately 30 minutes per screen update.

They decided to fix it by bringing in experts. They tweaked, upgraded
hardware, and so on. After a massive effort, the response rate had
improved to 15 minutes per screen. A significant improvement, but still a
useless system.

They ended up scrapping the project and going back to development
from scratch using a 3GL.

Object-Oriented Development

Object-oriented development especially when combined with component-based software development, does have the potential to significantly reduce costs. Development costs are typically decreased by roughly 10% (more if extensive reusable libraries are available). Even more spectacular, maintenance costs decrease by as much as 50%. Unfortunately, it is more difficult to design object-oriented systems, so good object-oriented designers are hard to come by.

Shackles and Whips

Of course, you can always rely on the old standbys of unpaid overtime, unrealistic schedules, and both formal and informal pressure to work extremely long hours. Unfortunately, the result often includes high staff turnover, poor quality, and resultant missed deadlines.

ADJUSTING CURVE COEFFICIENTS IN MORE DETAIL

It has been our experience that the quality of your development team has the biggest impact on how efficiently you develop a given volume of software, and hence affects the correct value for alpha for your organization. The key to adjusting your development efficiency is recognizing the tremendous difference in productivity between the best and the worst programmers (a factor of 10 to 25, depending on the environment). I find that programmers can be divided into three categories.

- *Average Programmer*—words like competent come to mind. Average programmers usually make up 80% of your staff.
- *Super Programmer*—words like guru and indispensable come to mind. Super programmers usually make up 10% of your staff.
- *Pitiful Programmer*—words like tries hard and cooperative come to mind. If not, then they would have been fired long ago. Pitiful programmers usually make up 10% of your staff.

Obviously, your objective is to have as many super programmers as possible. A company whose staff has 50% super programmers, rather than 10%, would be unstoppable!

The first rule is: Keep your super programmers at all costs. Whatever you pay, they are worth it.

Second, weed out the pitiful programmers and don't let them continue coding. That doesn't necessarily mean firing them. They are often quite good at non-developmental activities. Examples include testing, help desk support, and user training.

There are two basic approaches to increasing the percentage of super programmers on your staff.

1. Hire them.

    Good idea, but it won't work. Average and pitiful programmers are looking for work, not super programmers.

2. Grow your own.

    Keep your super programmers at all costs, work to turn your average programmers into super programmers, and identify and weed out the pitiful programmers.

Basically, this involves creating a work environment that is conducive to the development of super programmers. This involves optimizing the physical, mental, and professional growth environments.

OPTIMIZING THE PHYSICAL ENVIRONMENT

The key here is to ensure that the work environment is tailored to the needs of software developers. As a minimum, you should address internal and external interruptions, manuals and other reference materials, and the concept of a software library.

To understand the importance of minimizing interruptions, it is important that you first understand the concept of flow. This is the state of the human mind where it works at peak productivity. If you've ever worked on a task, then glanced up and realized that hours have passed, you were in a state of flow. Psychologists tell us that it takes between

20 and 30 minutes for the average individual to enter flow for an appropriate task. What does this say if there is an interruption every 20 minutes?

There are two basic flavors of repetitive interruptions: internal and external. Examples of internal interruptions include co-worker questions, meetings, and intercom systems. Examples of external interruptions include phone calls and customer or management demonstrations. It is critical that you look for ways to minimize the adverse impact of these interruptions. For example:

- Maximize the use of communication media that do not require an interruption (e.g., e-mail).
- Set aside periods of time during the day for interruption-free work.
- Break your work environment into areas that are designed for socialization, areas that are designed for cooperative work, and areas that are designed for non-interrupted work.
- Prepare canned demonstrations that can be presented to managers and customers with little or no involvement on the part of the programming team.

Certain reference manuals are used constantly by the development team. They should be within arm's reach of each programmer, either by putting them on-line or by purchasing enough individual copies for each programmer to keep them nearby. If you need to put software development standards on-line, you might want to consider a tool such as the HyperText Standards On-Line.

Good software librarians don't just maintain old, dusty code. They should be consultants to projects, advising programmers how to incorporate, use, and modify the corporation's code library (including internal code and external packages). The software librarian should be involved in the project from the early requirements definition stage all the way through the final delivery; and the librarian should be equally focused on ways to reuse existing code, and ways to design newly developed code to be more reusable.

OPTIMIZING THE MENTAL ENVIRONMENT

The following guidelines will help you ensure that you maintain a healthy development environment within your organization.

- Promote healthy competition. Use peer pressure and rewards.
- It must be clear that project success takes precedence over individual success. Everyone must work to make the team successful as a group.
- Communicate goals and the feelings behind the goals.
- Lead, but do not push.
- Provide liberal doses of responsibility.
- Trust your people.
- Forgive mistakes totally, but be ruthless when necessary. It is necessary to be ruthless in the event of outright rebellion, or when a single individual or clique is disruptive to the project as a whole.
- Overlook healthy conflict. Do not tolerate unhealthy conflict.

OPTIMIZING THE PROFESSIONAL GROWTH ENVIRONMENT

There are dozens of ways to encourage professional development without needing to have a big budget. This helps your programming staff become more skilled and increases morale. Here are some examples.

- Find evening classes or short duration day classes and help programmers register.
- Find and order (at company expense) appropriate books.
- Locate and subscribe to technical journals. For free journals, get one per programmer if possible.
- Check out appropriate technical books from libraries; loan them to programmers to read.
- Look for inexpensive PC software that teaches important skills.
- Encourage employees to use computers at night for school work and for experiments.

- Encourage employees to become in-house experts in skill areas.
- Assign employees tasks that use their new skills.

TRACKING COSTS

Reducing costs also requires that managers properly track project costs. The best tracking metrics look forward rather than backward. Backward metrics, such as funds expended to date, just tell you how you've done in the past. Predictors look forward and anticipate problems. Examples of descriptors are funds expended to date, funds remaining, and percent of code completed. Examples of predictors are projected completion date and projected total cost. Predictors are more useful than descriptors for project management and cost control.

The basic steps involved in tracking costs are:

1. Decomposing the project into tasks,
2. Assigning resources to the tasks,
3. Allocating hours or dollars to each task,
4. Tracking expenditures against the plan,
5. Tracking the percent complete, and
6. Calculating the plan versus budget for both dollars and time.

Cost•Xpert is designed to do tasks 1 and 3, and can help with task 2 by telling you the projected resource requirements for each phase of the project. Tasks 4, 5, and 6 must be managed using an external project management program. Cost•Xpert supports the export of a preliminary project plan into external project management programs to get you started.

The appendices to this manual describe some related software programs that are available, including: Risk•Xpert, a risk management tool that accepts Cost•Xpert risk data as an input; HyperText Standards On-Line, an on-line database of software development standards (including IEEE, DOD-STD-2167A, and MIL-STD-498); and Strategy•Xpert, a strategic planning tool that can be used to optimize organizational resources between projects that were estimated using Cost•Xpert.

QUICK START GUIDE

This appendix provides a fast introduction to the user interface and describes how to use key Cost•Xpert features. We describe how to start Cost•Xpert, then describe the application's main window and its components.

STARTING COST•XPERT

The easiest way to start Cost•Xpert is to double click on the Cost•Xpert icon within the Cost•Xpert program group. The CostXprt.exe Icon is displayed in Figure 37. If you are using Windows 95, you may wish to create a shortcut to Cost•Xpert on your desktop. See your Windows 95 documentation for the procedure to accomplish this task.

FIGURE 37 COST•XPERT ICON

After double clicking on the Cost•Xpert icon, the Cost•Xpert application main window will be displayed.

COST•XPERT MAIN WINDOW

If you have not already done so, start Cost•Xpert at this time. The Project Tab is the first screen to be viewed when Cost•Xpert is first opened. This section presents a quick overview of the main window components and application features.

Figure 38 displays the various components of the Cost•Xpert main window. Each component is discussed individually in the sections that follow.

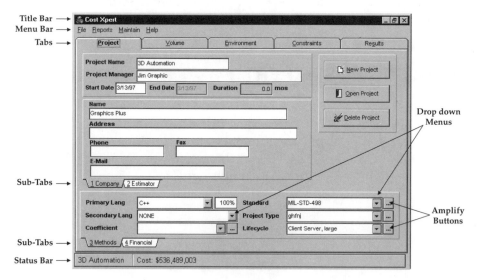

FIGURE 38 COST•XPERT MAIN WINDOW COMPONENTS

Title Bar

The Cost•Xpert title bar is located at the very top of the application window. This bar contains the system menu, minimize, maximize, and close buttons.

If you click on the system menu button (this is the icon of Cost•Xpert located on the upper left corner of the screen), it can perform the following menu options: Restore, Move, Size, Minimize, Maximize, and Close. Cost•Xpert can also be closed easily by double clicking on the system menu button.

Menu Bar

The Cost•Xpert Menu Bar appears at the top of the application screen just below the title bar. The menu bar displays the File, Reports, Maintain, and Help drop-down menus. The Cost•Xpert Menu choices are described in detail in the appendix called *Menu Choices*.

Status Bar

The Status Bar is located on the very bottom of the Cost•Xpert application window. This bar provides an easy reference to viewing project name, cost, and duration.

APPLICATION SCREEN FEATURES

This section will briefly review the Cost•Xpert application screen features including:

- Tabs,
- Sub-tabs,
- Grids,
- Scroll bars,
- Drop-down menus,
- Radio buttons, and
- Buttons.

Tabs

Cost•Xpert uses tabs to differentiate between the five main screens of the application. To select these tabs, click on the tab name that you wish to see. The contents of the tab will be displayed. Detailed information regarding each of the Cost•Xpert tabs is discussed in the Cost•Xpert *Screen Reference* appendix.

Sub-Tabs

Cost•Xpert uses sub-tabs located on the bottom section of the screen on the main tabs. These tabs allow additional screens to be viewed within a tab.

Grids

Most Cost•Xpert screens use grids to display information. All grid columns can be adjusted to increase or decrease the width displayed for the column. To accomplish this task, select the column bar separating the column from other columns and click and drag the bar until the desired width is accomplished. The grid will resize according to the new specifications. Additional information regarding these grids will be discussed in the Cost•Xpert *Screen Reference* appendix.

Scroll Bars

Like other Windows applications, Cost•Xpert uses scroll bars to view data in grids which exceed the size of the screen. Click on the up and down or right and left arrows located on scroll bars to view additional data.

Drop-Down Menus

Cost•Xpert uses drop-down menus to display menu choices. Menus contain function and hot keys to display information. For a detailed reference to all Cost•Xpert menus, refer to the *Menu Choices* appendix.

Radio Buttons

Cost•Xpert uses radio buttons to select a specific option in the application. Some screens have dual views of *New* and *Reused.* By clicking on the corresponding radio button, the user can specify either option.

Buttons

Cost•Xpert uses buttons to perform specific functions. The *Screen Reference* appendix provides a complete overview of all Cost•Xpert buttons.

B

appendix

Menu Choices

This section illustrates and describes the Cost•Xpert menu choices.

FILE MENU

The File Menu contains the menu choices that are displayed in Figure 39. Projects can be created, opened, and deleted from the file menu.

File/Change Data Directory

Select **File/Change Data Directory** from the drop-down menu to specify a different data directory.

File/Change Temp Directory

To change the Temp directory, select the corresponding menu choice and specify a new Temp directory.

File/Export to Microsoft Project

To export project data from Cost•Xpert to Microsoft Project, select

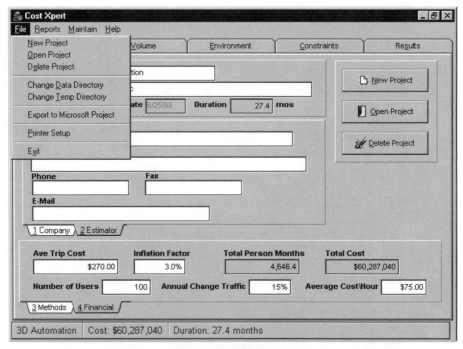

FIGURE 39 FILE MENU

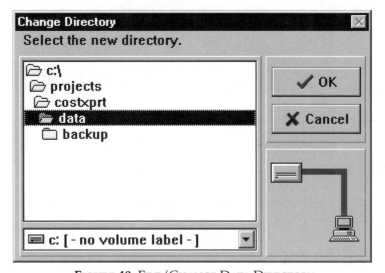

FIGURE 40 FILE/CHANGE DATA DIRECTORY

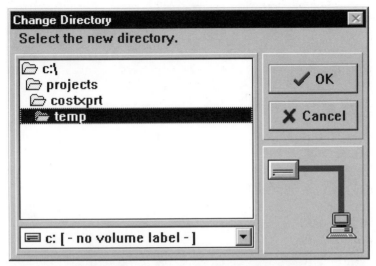

FIGURE 41 FILE/CHANGE TEMP DIRECTORY

File/Export to Microsoft Project menu choice. Save the file as a TEXT (*.TXT) file and name it according to the project.

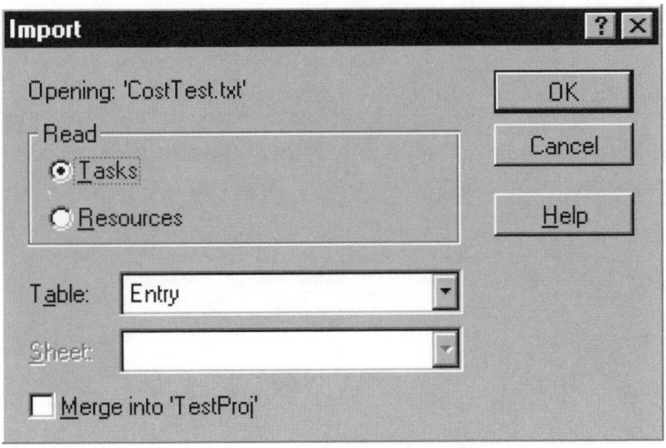

FIGURE 42 FILE/EXPORT TO MICROSOFT PROJECT

Opening a File in Microsoft Project

To open an exported Cost•Xpert file in Microsoft Project, use the following steps:

1. Start Microsoft Project.
2. Select **Open** from the File menu in Microsoft Project.
3. Select the path and file name of the exported Cost•Xpert *.TXT file.
4. Open the text file.

Once the text file is open, the file will need to be imported into Microsoft Project.

FIGURE 43 OPENING A FILE IN MICROSOFT PROJECT

Importing to Microsoft Project

To import a file into Microsoft Project:

1. Select **Import** from the Microsoft Project File menu.

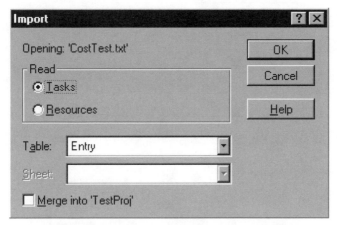

FIGURE 44 IMPORTING TO MICROSOFT PROJECT

2. Select *Tasks*.

3. Select a table.

4. Click **OK** and the data from the Cost•Xpert project will be imported into Microsoft Project.

REPORTS MENU

The Reports Menu allows a user to run the various reports in Cost•Xpert. Detailed information about all Cost•Xpert Reports is described in the *Reports* appendix.

MAINTAIN MENU

The Maintain Menu allows the user to access various screens relevant to the project. The following sections describe each of the Maintain Menu choices.

The following Maintain Menu choices can also be accessed by using the Amplify/Edit button located on the Project Tab, Methods Sub-Tab:

- Coefficients,
- Standard,
- Project Type, and
- Life cycle.

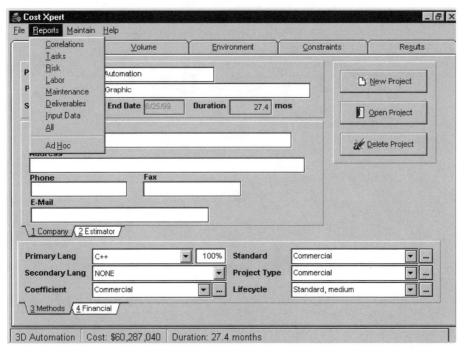

FIGURE 45 REPORTS MENU

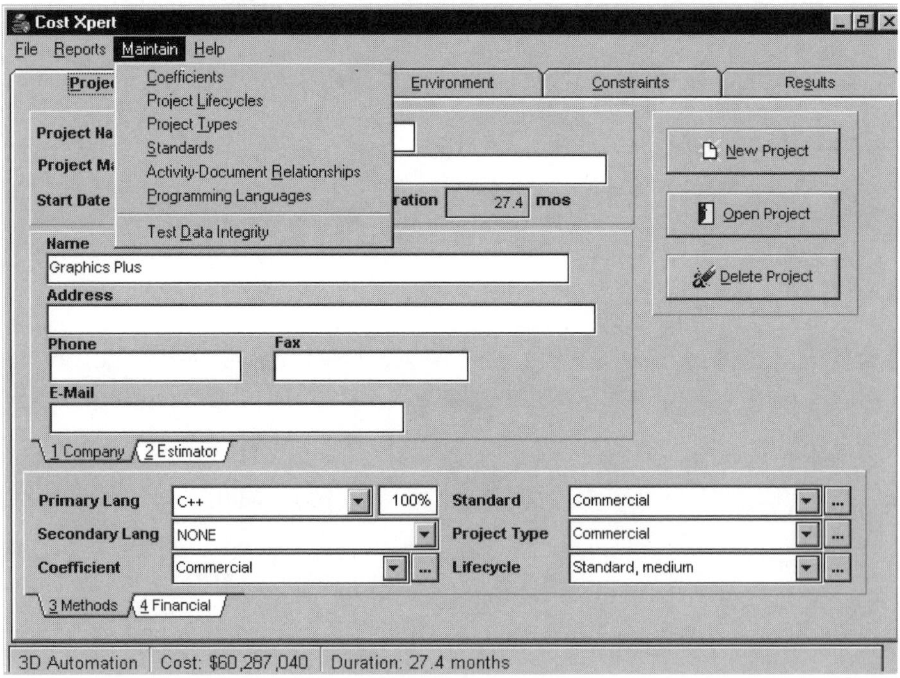

FIGURE 46 MAINTAIN MENU

Maintain/Coefficients

The Maintain/Coefficients screen displays the following information relevant to the project:

- Name,
- M(A),
- M(B),
- T(A),
- T(B),
- Calculation for Effort, and
- Calculation for Optimal Time.

Coefficients can be added and deleted from the Maintain/Coefficients screen.

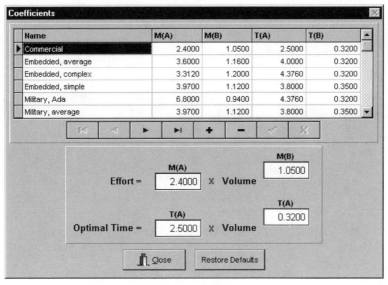

FIGURE 47 MAINTAIN/COEFFICIENTS

Maintain/Project Life Cycles

The Maintain/Project Life cycle screen allows the user to select the type of project life cycle relevant to the type of project being defined. A description for each type of life cycle is displayed on the screen. Activities and descriptions that fall into the life-cycle type are also displayed. The user can add or delete activities and specify the project phase to which the activities pertain.

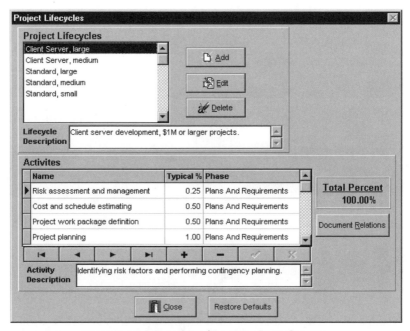

FIGURE 48 MAINTAIN/PROJECT LIFE CYCLES

Maintain/Project Types, Likely Risks Sub-Tab

The Maintain/Project Types screen has three sub-tabs:

- Likely Risks,
- Defects, and
- Support Calls.

Figure 49 Maintain/Project Types, Likely Risks Sub-Tab

The Likely Risks Sub-Tab provides information about the project risks. A predefined list of risks is displayed according to the project type. Each type has a different set of risks. For new project types specified by the user, a new set of risks can also be specified. All risks can be adjusted according to the user's needs for the project.

Maintain/Project Types, Likely Defects Sub-Tab

The Project Types, Defects Sub-Tab displays defect information for each project type. This information can be adjusted according to the user's needs for the project.

Maintain/Project Types, Likely Support Calls Sub-Tab

The Support Calls Sub-Tab displays the expected support calls per year for each of the project types. The user can adjust these estimates based on the project needs.

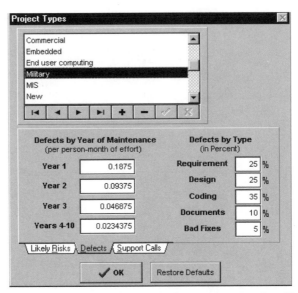

Figure 50 Maintain/Project Types, Defects Sub-Tab

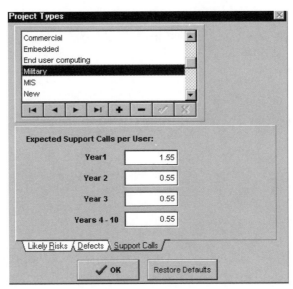

Figure 51 Maintain/Project Types, Support Calls Sub-Tab

Maintain/Standards

The Maintain/Standards screen displays a set of predefined documents and descriptions for each of the standards in Cost•Xpert.

Documents can be added or deleted according to the user's needs.

An existing project standard can be duplicated and renamed to use as a basis for a new standard type. The documents within that standard can then be tailored (by adding or deleting) to the new standard type. This is accomplished by selecting the desired master standard and selecting the Duplicate button on the right side of the screen. Name the standard accordingly and tailor the documents to the new standard needs.

The Restore Defaults button can be selected to restore the standards back to the original settings defined in Cost•Xpert.

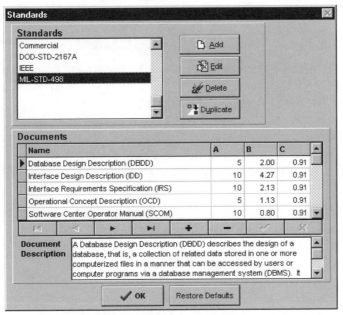

FIGURE 52 MAINTAIN/STANDARDS

Maintain/Activity-Document Relationships

The Maintain/Activity-Document Relationships screen is used to display and establish affiliations between project Life cycles, Standards, Activities, and Documents.

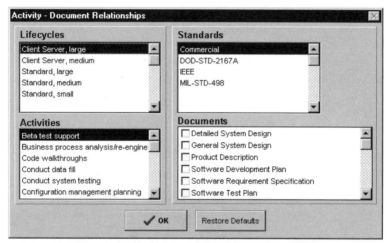

FIGURE 53 MAINTAIN/ACTIVITY-DOCUMENT RELATIONSHIPS

Maintain/Programming Languages

The Maintain/Programming Languages screen displays the programming languages and function points to equivalent source lines-of-code referenced in Cost•Xpert. New languages can be added and old ones can be deleted. Function points can also be adjusted.

If a mistake is made, the Restore Defaults button can be used to refresh the original Cost•Xpert settings for this screen.

Maintain/Test Data Integrity

The Test Data Integrity screen checks the database for corrupted files. This menu selection runs a utility to verify that all is well with the data files in Cost•Xpert.

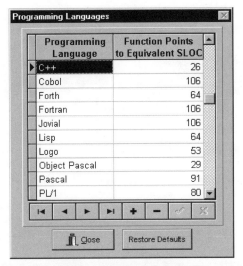

FIGURE 54 MAINTAIN/PROGRAMMING LANGUAGES

FIGURE 55 MAINTAIN/TEST DATA INTEGRITY

HELP MENU

The Help menu is discussed in the sections that follow.

Help/Contacting Marotz

This menu choice displays information on how to contact Marotz.

Help/About

The Help/About menu choice allows the user to view the version and copyright information for Cost•Xpert.

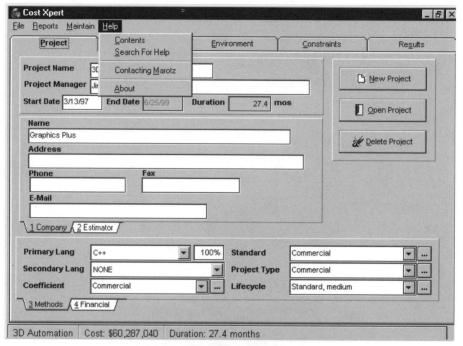

FIGURE 56 HELP MENU

FIGURE 57 HELP/CONTACTING MAROTZ

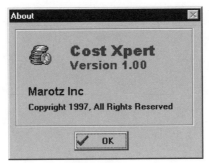

FIGURE 58 HELP/ABOUT

C
appendix

Screen Reference

As discussed in the *Quick Start Guide* appendix, start Cost•Xpert by double-clicking on the Cost•Xpert Icon. The application will begin running in full-screen mode.

Cost•Xpert consists of five main tabs:

- Project,
- Volume,
- Environment,
- Constraints, and
- Results.

Illustrations and detailed information regarding the purpose, context, content, and use of each of the screens in Cost•Xpert will be discussed in the sections that follow.

PROJECT TAB

The Project Tab is the first screen displayed in Cost•Xpert. Components of the Project Tab are described below.

Company Sub-Tab

The Project Tab, Company Sub-Tab is illustrated and described in the section that follows.

Purpose

The purpose of the Project Tab, Company Sub-Tab is to display information about the company.

Context

The Project Tab, Company Sub-Tab is located in the center of the Cost•Xpert Project screen. The Company Sub-Tab is indicated by the number 1 located to the left of the sub-tab name.

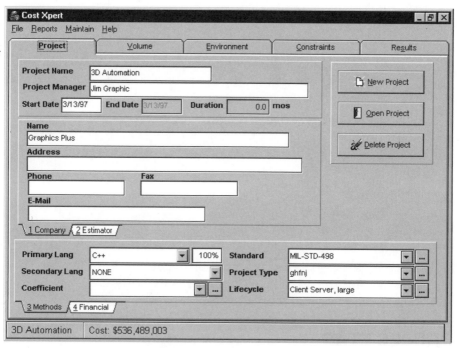

FIGURE 59 PROJECT TAB, COMPANY SUB-TAB

Content and Use

This screen contains information relevant to the company. Name, address, phone, fax, and e-mail for the company can be entered.

Estimator Sub-Tab

The Project Tab, Estimator Sub-Tab is illustrated and described below (Figure 60).

Purpose

The purpose of the Project Tab, Estimator Sub-Tab is to provide information about the estimator.

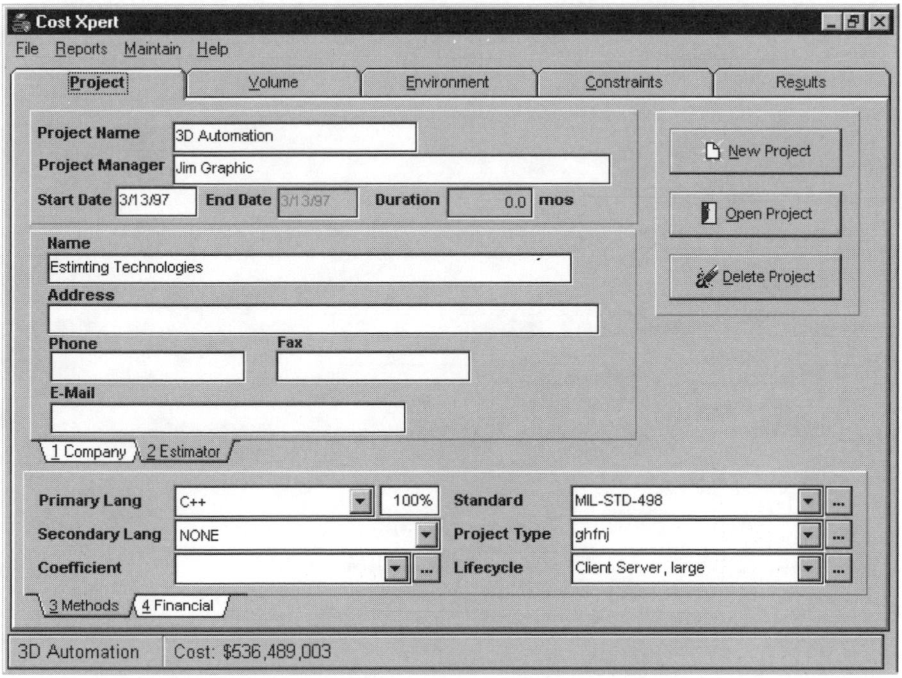

FIGURE 60 PROJECT TAB, ESTIMATOR SUB-TAB

Context

The Project Tab, Estimator Sub-Tab is located in the center of the Cost•Xpert Project screen. The Estimator Sub-Tab is indicated by the number 2 located to the left of the sub-tab name.

Content and Use

This screen provides information about the estimator. Name, address, phone, fax, and e-mail contact information for the estimator can be entered on this sub-tab.

Methods Sub-Tab

The Project Tab, Methods Sub-Tab is illustrated and described in the section that follows (see Figure 61).

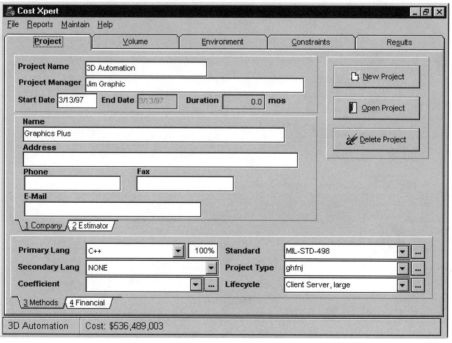

FIGURE 61 PROJECT TAB, METHODS SUB-TAB

Purpose

The Project Tab, Methods Sub-Tab contains important information relevant to the project. This tab allows the user to specify project languages, coefficients, standards, project type, and life cycle.

Context

The Project Tab, Methods Sub-Tab is located near the bottom of the Cost•Xpert Project screen. The Methods Sub-Tab is indicated by the number 3 located to the left of the sub-tab name.

Content and Use

The Methods Sub-Tab is used to define important information about the project.

- The user can chose a Primary Programming Language from the drop-down pick list. A percentage of the primary programming language used can also be specified by the user.
- A secondary Language can also be chosen from the drop-down pick list.
- Project Coefficients can be chosen from a drop-down pick list. By clicking on the Coefficient Amplify/Edit button, the user can access the Maintain/Coefficients screen. For details on the Maintain/Coefficients screen, refer to the *Menu Choices* appendix.
- Project Standards can be chosen from the drop-down pick list. By clicking on the Standards Amplify/Edit button, the user can access the Maintain/Standards screen. For details on the Maintain/Standards screen, refer to the *Menu Choices* appendix.
- Project Type can also be chosen by selecting the type from the drop-down pick list. By clicking on the Project Type Amplify/Edit button, the user can access the Maintain/Project Type screen. For details on the Maintain/Project Type screen, refer to the *Menu Choices* appendix.

- Project Life cycle can also be chosen by selecting the life-cycle type from the drop-down pick list. By clicking on the Life Cycle Amplify/Edit button, the user can access the Maintain/Life Cycle screen. For details on the Maintain/Life Cycle screen, refer to the *Menu Choices* appendix.

Financial Sub-Tab

The Project Tab, Financial Sub-Tab is illustrated and described in the section that follows (see Figure 62).

Purpose

The Project Tab, Financial Sub-Tab contains important financial information relevant to the project. This tab allows the user to specify financial information about the project.

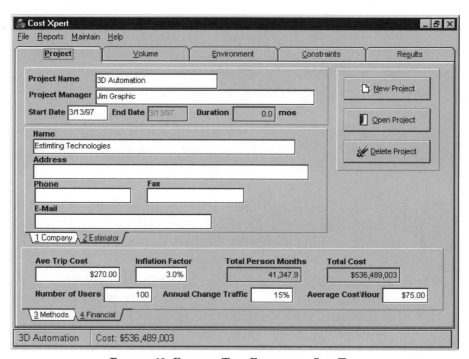

FIGURE 62 PROJECT TAB, FINANCIAL SUB-TAB

Context

The Project Tab, Financial Sub-Tab is located near the bottom of the Cost•Xpert Project screen. The Financial Sub-Tab is indicated by the number 4 located to the left of the sub-tab name.

Content and Use

The Financial Sub-Tab is used to define important financial information about the project. The user can define information for:

- Average trip cost,
- Inflation factor percentage,
- Number of users of project,
- Annual change traffic percentage, and
- Average cost per hour.

  Additionally, the user can view:

- Total projected person months, and
- Total projected project cost.

VOLUME TAB

The Volume Tab is the second main tab displayed in Cost•Xpert. Components of the Volume Tab are described in the sections that follow.

SLOC Sub-Tab, New Type

The Volume Tab, SLOC Sub-Tab, New Type screen is illustrated and described in the section that follows (see Figure 63).

Purpose

The Volume Tab, SLOC Sub-Tab, New Type, provides information about the number of new source lines-of-code.

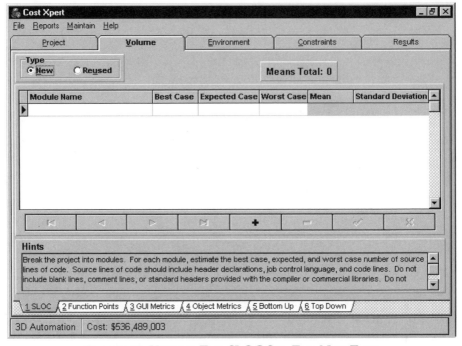

FIGURE 63 VOLUME TAB, SLOC SUB-TAB, NEW TYPE

Context

This screen can be accessed by selecting the number 1 SLOC Sub-Tab from the main Volume Tab.

Content and Use

The SLOC Sub-Tab, New Type screen can be used to define modules and to estimate best, expected, and worst case source lines-of-code for each of the modules. Cost•Xpert will calculate the mean and standard deviation for each of the modules defined by the user. Cost•Xpert provides hints that the user can take into consideration when estimating source lines-of-code.

The "+" button, located in the center of the screen below the grid, is used to add new modules. For further information on scrolling through, deleting, and posting modules from the button tool bar on this screen, refer to the *Menu Choices* appendix.

SLOC Sub-Tab, Reused Type

The Volume Tab, SLOC Sub-Tab, Reused Type screen is illustrated and described in the section that follows (see Figure 64).

Purpose

The Volume Tab, SLOC Sub-Tab, Reused Type provides reused module information for source lines-of-code.

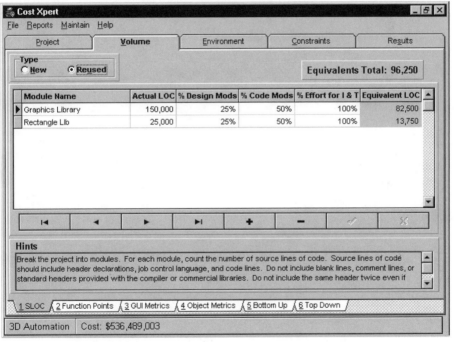

FIGURE 64 VOLUME TAB, SLOC SUB-TAB, REUSED TYPE

Context

Select this screen by clicking on the SLOC Sub-Tab, Volume Tab, and selecting the *Reused* radio button.

Content and Use

This screen provides information about modules with reused source lines-of-code.

For details about the functionality of this screen refer to the *Volume Tab, SLOC Sub-Tab* section of this appendix.

Function Points Sub-Tab, New Type

The Volume Tab, Function Points Sub-Tab, New Type screen is illustrated and described in the section that follows (see Figure 65).

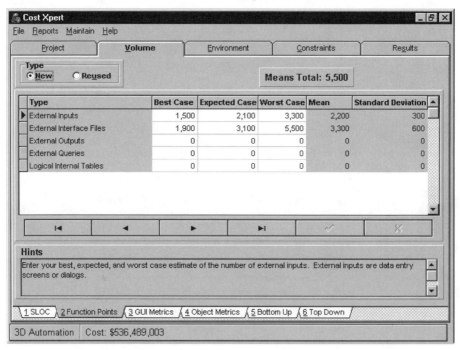

FIGURE 65 VOLUME TAB, FUNCTION POINTS SUB-TAB, NEW TYPE

Purpose

The purpose of the Volume Tab, Function Points Sub-Tab, New Type is to provide information regarding project function points.

Context

Access this screen by selecting the Function Point Sub-Tab from the main Volume Tab and selecting the *New Type* radio button.

Content and Use

This screen is used to provide information about Function Points. Function Points will be predefined so that the user can input data estimates for the best, expected, and worst case for each function point. A panel containing hints for each of the selected function point types is provided to facilitate the user in estimating the level of effort for each function point. Select the "√" to complete input of estimate.

Cost•Xpert will calculate the Mean, Standard Deviation, and Means Total for the New Function Points.

Function Points Sub-Tab, Reused Type

The Volume Tab, Function Points Sub-Tab, Reused Type screen is illustrated and described in the section that follows (see Figure 66).

Purpose

The Volume Tab, Function Points Sub-Tab, Reused Type provides information about Reused Function Points.

Context

Access this screen by selecting the Function Points Sub-Tab, main Volume Tab, and clicking on the *Reused* radio button.

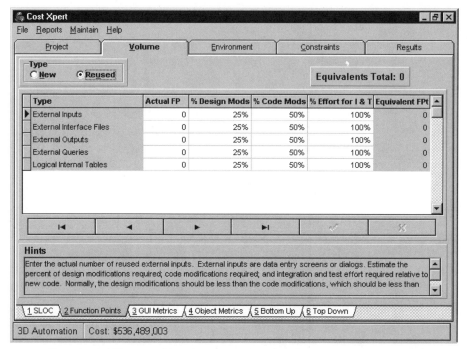

FIGURE 66 VOLUME TAB, FUNCTION POINTS SUB-TAB, REUSED TYPE

Content and Use

This screen provides information about Reused Function Points. The user needs to enter the actual number for each of the predefined Function Points. The user then needs to enter an estimate for the percentage of Design Mods, Code Mods, and Effort for I & T for each function point type. Cost•Xpert will then calculate an Equivalents Total and Equivalents Function Point.

GUI Metrics Sub-Tab, New Type

The Volume Tab, GUI Metrics Sub-Tab, New Type screen is illustrated and described in the following section (see Figure 67).

Purpose

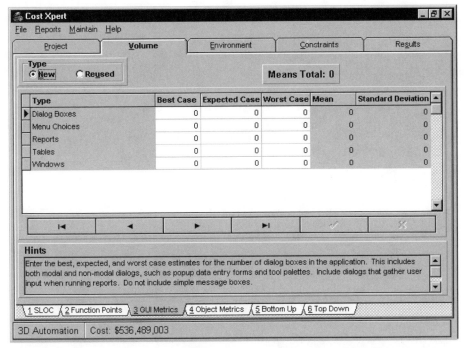

FIGURE 67 VOLUME TAB, GUI METRICS SUB-TAB, NEW TYPE

The Volume Tab, GUI Metrics Sub-Tab, New Type screen provides information regarding new GUI Metrics.

Context

Access this screen by selecting the GUI Metrics Sub-Tab from the main Volume Tab and select the *New Type* radio button.

Content and Use

The Volume Tab, GUI Metrics Sub-Tab provides information about new GUI Metrics. Cost•Xpert provides several types of predefined GUI Metrics. The user needs to enter best, expected, and worst case estimates for the number of each type of GUI Metric defined by Cost•Xpert. After the user inputs their data, Cost•Xpert will calculate the Mean, Standard

Deviation, and Means Total for New GUI Metrics.

Cost•Xpert provides helpful hints to the user to facilitate input data on the various sub-tabs of the Volume Tab. These hints are located near the bottom of the screen on each of the sub-tabs.

GUI Metrics Sub-Tab, Reused Type

The Volume Tab, GUI Metrics Sub-Tab, Reused Type screen is illustrated and described in the section that follows (see Figure 68).

Purpose

The Volume Tab, GUI Metrics Sub-Tab, Reused Type screen provides information regarding reused GUI Metrics.

Context

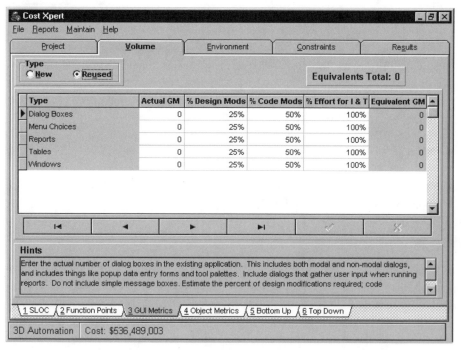

FIGURE 68 VOLUME TAB, GUI METRICS SUB-TAB, REUSED TAB

Access this screen by selecting the GUI Metrics Sub-Tab from the main Volume Tab and selecting the *Reused Type* radio button.

Content and Use

The Volume Tab, GUI Metrics Sub-Tab, Reused Type provides information regarding reused GUI Metrics. A table with predefined GUI metric types is found in the center of the screen. The user can input data pertaining to actual GUI Metrics, percentages of Design Mods, Code Mods, and Effort for I & T. Cost•Xpert will calculate the Equivalents Total and Equivalent Number of GUI Metrics for the reused GUI Metrics.

Like the Volume Tab, GUI Metrics Sub-Tab, New Type, the Reused Type screen provides hints pertaining to Reused GUI Metrics.

Object Metrics Sub-Tab, New Type

The Volume Tab, Object Metrics Sub-Tab, New Type screen is illustrated and described in the following section (see Figure 69).

Purpose

The Volume Tab, Object Metrics Sub-Tab, New Type screen provides information regarding new Object Metrics.

Context

Access this screen by selecting the Volume Tab, Object Metrics Sub-Tab, and clicking on the *New Type* radio button.

Content and Use

The Volume Tab, Object Metrics Sub-Tab, New Type screen displays information relevant to new Object Metrics. The user can input information for the best, expected, and worst case for each of the predefined New Object Metric Types. Once this information is provided, Cost•Xpert will calculate the Means Total, Mean, and Standard Deviation for New Object Metrics applicable to the project.

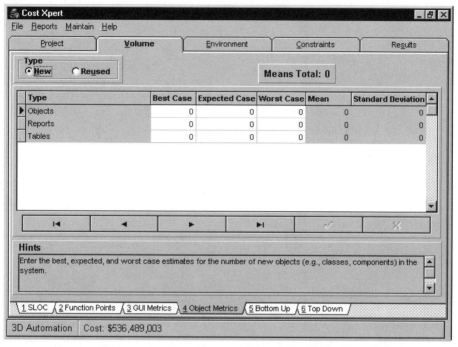

FIGURE 69 VOLUME TAB, OBJECT METRICS SUB-TAB, NEW TYPE

Object Metrics Sub-Tab, Reused Type

The Volume Tab, Object Metrics Sub-Tab, Reused Type screen is illustrated and described in the section that follows (see Figure 70).

Purpose

The Volume Tab, GUI Metrics Sub-Tab, Reused Type screen provides information regarding reused GUI Metrics.

Context

Access this screen by selecting the Volume Tab, Object Metrics Sub-Tab, and clicking on the *Reused* radio button.

Content and Use

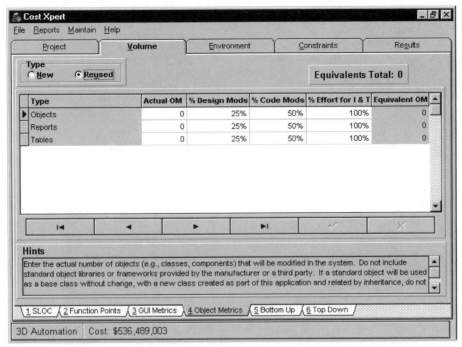

FIGURE 70 VOLUME TAB, OBJECT METRICS SUB-TAB, REUSED TYPE

The Reused Type Object Metric Sub-Tab provides information about reused object metrics. As required in the New Type Object Metrics Sub-Tab, the user must input information relevant to the Reused Type. The actual OM and percentages for Design Mods, Code Mods, and Effort for I & T need to be completed by the user. Cost•Xpert will then make calculations based on the user's input.

A hint is provided on the bottom of the screen for each of the Object Metric types.

Bottom Up Sub-Tab, New Type

The Volume Tab, Bottom Up Sub-Tab, New Type screen is illustrated and described in the section that follows (see Figure 71).

Purpose

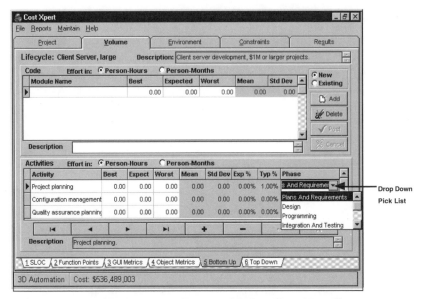

FIGURE 71 VOLUME TAB, BOTTOM UP SUB-TAB, NEW TYPE

The Volume Tab, Bottom Up Sub-Tab, New Type screen provides information regarding new Bottom Up information.

Context

Access this screen by selecting the Volume Tab, Bottom Up Sub-Tab, and
clicking on the *New Type* radio button.

Content and Use

The Volume Tab, Bottom Up Sub-Tab, New Type screen displays new Bottom Up information about the project. At the top of the screen, the project lifecycle and description are displayed. The top part of the Bottom Up
Sub-Tab screen provides information relevant to the code.

First of all, the user can specify whether the project effort should be
in Person Hours or Person Months. This is specified by selecting the des-
ignated radio button.

New modules can be added by selecting the Add button in the upper right section of the screen. Once Module Name is entered, a description can also be added for that particular module. The user needs to input best, expected, and worst case person-hour or person-month estimates for the specific module. Additional modules can be added if necessary.

The bottom half of the screen pertains to project activities. The project activities can also be measured in person hours or person months. Cost•Xpert provides a set of predefined activities to facilitate the user. Activities can be added or deleted at the user's discretion. The user needs to input best, expected, and worst case time estimates for each activity.

Finally, the user needs to determine the phase in which the specified activity is relevant. This is done by dropping down the activity phase pick list and selecting the appropriate phase from the list.

Bottom Up Sub-Tab, Existing Type

The Volume Tab, Bottom Up Sub-Tab, Existing Type screen is illustrated and described in the following section (see Figure 72).

Purpose

The Volume Tab, Bottom Up Sub-Tab, Existing Type screen provides information regarding Existing Bottom Up information.

Context

Access this screen by selecting the Bottom Up Sub-Tab from the main Volume Tab and clicking on the *Existing Type* radio button.

Content and Use

The Bottom Up Sub-Tab, Existing Type screen contains existing code and activity bottom up information about the project. The user can elaborate and build on the examples that Cost•Xpert provides. The user can specify information pertaining to the existing code modules and activities. New ones can be added and irrelevant ones can be deleted. Activity phase can also be specified.

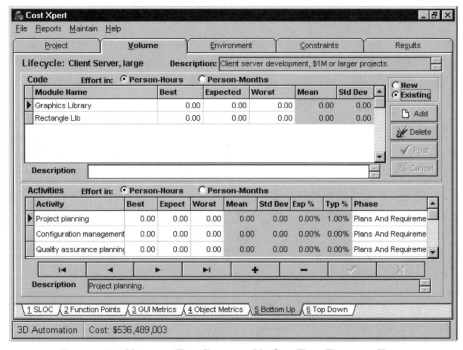

FIGURE 72 VOLUME TAB, BOTTOM UP SUB-TAB, EXISTING TYPE

Top Down Sub-Tab

The Volume Tab, Top Down Sub-Tab is illustrated and described in the following section (see Figure 73).

Purpose

The Volume Tab, Top Down Sub-Tab provides Top Down information about the project.

Context

Access this screen by selecting the Top Down Sub-Tab from the main Volume Tab.

Content and Use

The Top Down Sub-Tab provides information about the project and its

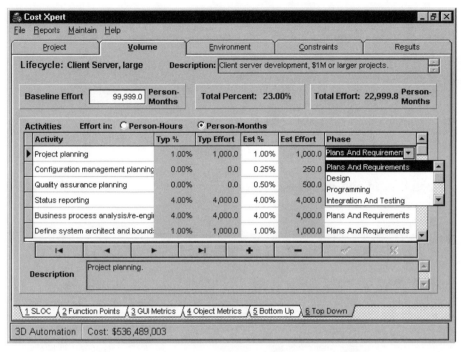

FIGURE 73 VOLUME TAB, TOP DOWN SUB-TAB

activities. At the top of the screen, the project lifecycle and description are displayed. The Baseline Effort needs to be input by the user. Activities can be added or deleted from the Top Down Sub-Tab. The user can specify the estimated percentage and Phase for each activity. Based on the user's input, Cost•Xpert makes many calculations which are displayed on this screen.

ENVIRONMENT TAB

The Environment Tab is the third main tab displayed in Cost•Xpert. Components of the Environment Tab are described in the following sections.

Experience Sub-Tab

The Environment Tab, Experience Sub-Tab is illustrated and described in the section that follows (see Figure 74).

Purpose

The Environment Tab, Experience Sub-Tab provides information about the experience factors of the project.

Context

Access this screen by selecting the Experience Sub-Tab from the main Environment Tab.

Content and Use

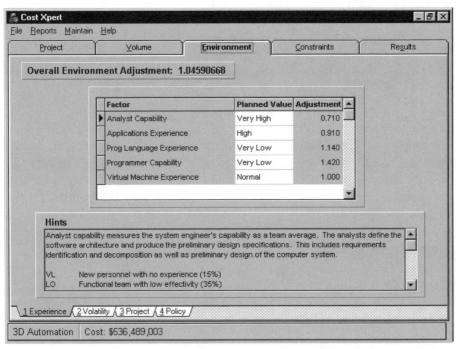

FIGURE 74 ENVIRONMENT TAB, EXPERIENCE SUB-TAB

This screen provides a list of predefined experience factors which will affect the outcome of the project. The user needs to specify a Planned Value for each of the Experience Factors. Planned Value drop-down menu selections for each factor are:

- Very Low,
- Low,
- Normal,
- High, and
- Very High.

Hints are provided on the bottom of the screen to facilitate the user in assigning a planned value for each of the experience factors. Once the information is input from the user, Cost•Xpert calculates the Overall Environment Adjustment and Adjustment per Factor.

Volatility Sub-Tab

The Environment Tab, Volatility Sub-Tab is illustrated and described in the section that follows (see Figure 75).

Purpose

The Environment Tab, Volatility Sub-Tab provides information about the project.

Context

Access this screen by selecting the Volatility Sub-Tab from the main Environment Tab.

Content and Use

This screen provides a list of predefined volatility factors which will affect the outcome of the project. The user needs to specify a planned value for each of the predefined volatility factors. Cost•Xpert will take the planned values specified by the user and calculate the overall environment

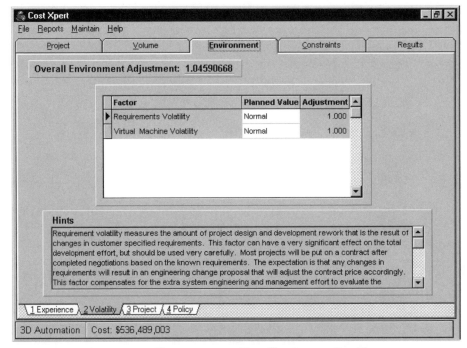

FIGURE 75 ENVIRONMENT TAB, VOLATILITY SUB-TAB

adjustment.

Project Sub-Tab

The Environment Tab, Project Sub-Tab is illustrated and described in the section that follows (see Figure 76).

Purpose

The Environment Tab, Project Sub-Tab provides environmental project information.

Context

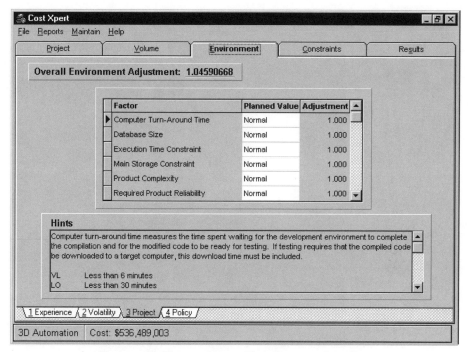

FIGURE 76 ENVIRONMENT TAB, PROJECT SUB-TAB

Access this screen by selecting the Project Sub-Tab from the Environment Tab.

Content and Use

This screen displays a list of the predefined project factors for which the user needs to specify a planned value. Hints are provided to facilitate the user. An overall environmental adjustment will be calculated based on the user's input.

Policy Sub-Tab

The Environment Tab, Policy Sub-Tab is illustrated and described in the section that follows (see Figure 77).

Purpose

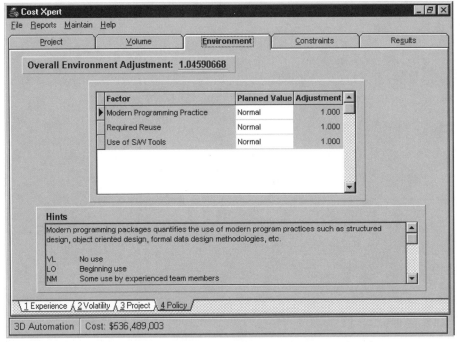

FIGURE 77 ENVIRONMENT TAB, POLICY SUB-TAB

The Environment Tab, Policy Sub-Tab provides environmental policy information about the project.

Context

Access this screen by selecting the Policy Sub-Tab from the main Environment Tab.

Content and Use

This screen provides environmental information about the policies of the project. A list of predefined policy factors are displayed so the user can assess planned values. Hints are provided so the user can easily understand if the policy factors are applicable to the project. Cost•Xpert will calculate an overall environmental adjustment based on the user's input.

CONSTRAINTS TAB

The Constraints Tab is illustrated and described in the section that follows (see Figure 78).

Purpose

The Constraints Tab provides information pertaining to project constraints.

Context

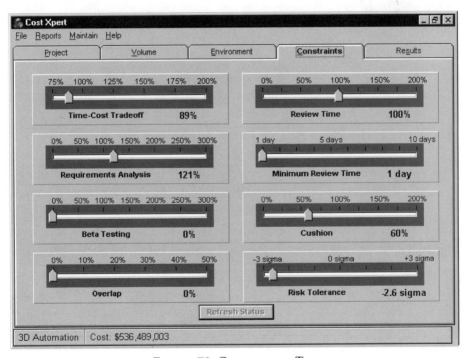

FIGURE 78 CONSTRAINTS TAB

Access this screen by selecting the Constraints Tab.

Content and Use

The user can use the Constraints Tab to assign a numerical value to eight constraint areas relevant to the specified project. The areas that the user can assess are:

- Time/cost trade-off,
- Review time,
- Requirements analysis,
- Minimum review time,
- Beta testing,
- Cushion,
- Overlap, and
- Risk tolerance.

The estimated percentage that the user assigns to each of the constraint areas is shown on the bottom of each of the percentage meters.

RESULTS TAB

The Results Tab is the last main tab displayed in Cost•Xpert. Components of the Results Tab are described below (see Figure 79).

Correlation Sub-Tab

The Results Tab, Correlation Sub-Tab is illustrated and described in the section that follows.

Purpose

The Results Tab, Correlation Sub-Tab provides correlating results about the project.

Context

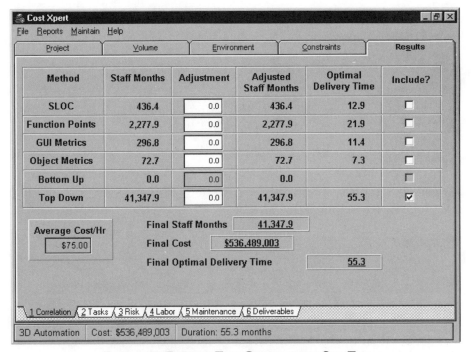

FIGURE 79 RESULTS TAB, CORRELATION SUB-TAB

Access this screen by selecting the Correlation Sub-Tab from the main Results Tab.

Content and Use

The Results Tab, Correlation Sub-Tab provides the following information about the project:

- Method,
- Staff months,
- Adjustment,
- Adjusted staff months,
- Optimal delivery time,
- Average cost per hour,

- Final staff months,
- Final cost, and
- Final delivery time.

The user can specify an adjustment for the staff months for each of the methods of the project. The user can also specify if methods should be included in the results of the project or not.

Tasks Sub-Tab

The Results Tab, Tasks Sub-Tab is illustrated and described in the section that follows (see Figure 80).

Purpose

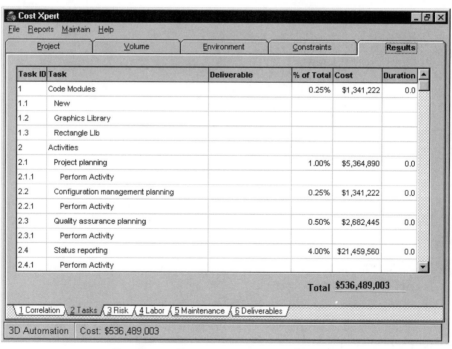

FIGURE 80 RESULTS TAB, TASKS SUB-TAB

The Results Tab, Tasks Sub-Tab provides information about the task results.

Context

Access this screen by selecting the Tasks Sub-Tab from the main Results Tab.

Content and Use

The Tasks screen provides the following information for the user to view:

- Task ID,
- Task,
- Deliverable,
- Percent of Total,
- Cost,
- Duration, and
- Total Project Cost.

Risk Sub-Tab

The Results Tab, Risk Sub-Tab is illustrated and described in the section that follows (see Figure 81).

Purpose

The Results Tab, Risk Sub-Tab contains information pertaining to the risk results.

Context

Access this screen by selecting the Risk Sub-Tab from the main Results Tab.

Content and Use

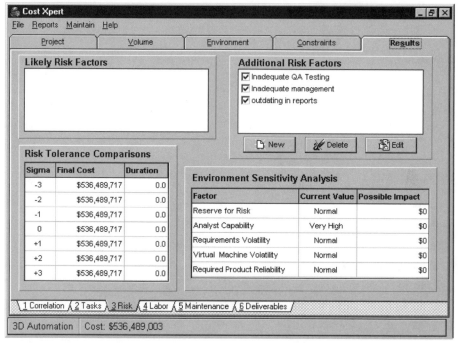

FIGURE 81 RESULTS TAB, RISK SUB-TAB

The Risk Sub-Tab provides risk information about the project. There are four areas to the Risk Sub-Tab.

1. Likely risk factors,
2. Additional risk factors,
3. Risk tolerance comparisons, and
4. Environment sensitivity analysis.

The user can select the Likely Risk Factors that are applicable to the specified project. The unchecked risk factors will not be included in the project risk calculations.

The user can add or delete Additional Risk Factors.

The Risk Tolerance Analysis and Environment Sensitivity Analysis display information relevant to the project risk factors.

Labor Sub-Tab

The Results Tab, Labor Sub-Tab is illustrated and described in the following section (see Figure 82).

Purpose

The Results Tab, Labor Sub-Tab contains information about the labor results for the project.

Context

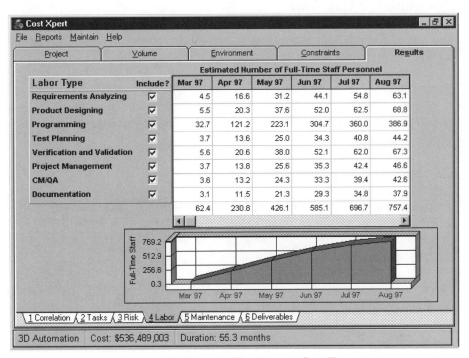

FIGURE 82 RESULTS TAB, LABOR SUB-TAB

Access this screen by selecting the Labor Sub-Tab from the main Results Tab.

Content and Use

The Labor Sub-Tab displays Labor Type and the Estimated Number of Full Time Staff Personnel. The user can specify the labor types required for the project analysis. This is done by clicking on the check box associated with the desired labor types.

The bottom of the screen contains a graph displaying the number of full-time staff for the projected project duration.

Maintenance Sub-Tab

The Results Tab, Maintenance Sub-Tab is illustrated and described in the section that follows (see Figure 83).

Purpose

The Results Tab, Maintenance Sub-Tab provides information about maintenance results.

Context

Access this screen by selecting the Maintenance Sub-Tab from the main Results Tab.

Content and Use

The Maintenance Sub-Tab displays the following information about the results:

- Number of users,
- Annual change traffic,
- Year,
- Labor,
- Costs,

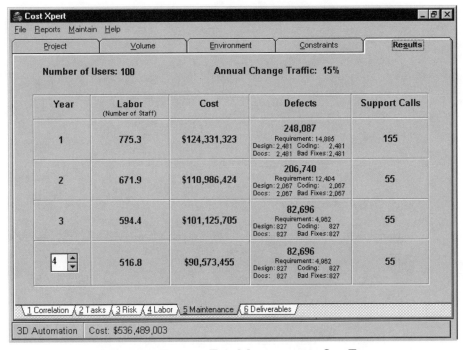

FIGURE 83 RESULTS TAB, MAINTENANCE SUB-TAB

- Defects, and
- Support Calls.

The user can scroll all the way to 10 years to see the maintenance projections for the project.

Deliverables Sub-Tab

The Results Tab, Deliverables Sub-Tab is illustrated and described in the section that follows (see Figure 84).

Purpose

The Results Tab, Deliverables Sub-Tab provides information regarding the results for the project.

Context

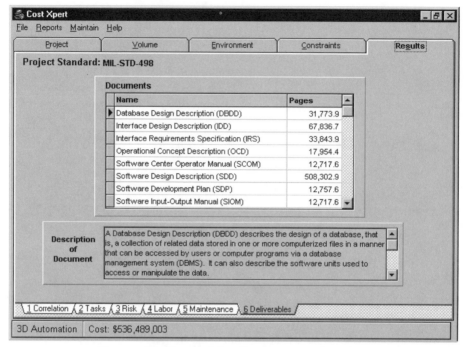

FIGURE 84 RESULTS TAB, DELIVERABLES SUB-TAB

Access this screen by selecting the Deliverables Sub-Tab from the main Results Tab.

Content and Use

The Deliverables Sub-Tab displays the document name, pages of the document, and description of the document deliverables for the project.

appendix

D

REPORTS

This appendix covers Cost•Xpert Reports. All reports in Cost•Xpert contain a report title, a project name, and a footer containing the date and time the report was prepared. In addition, most reports contain the estimated duration and estimated cost of the project.

CORRELATION

The Correlation report is displayed in Figure 85. This report displays the following field information:

- Estimating method,
- Staff months,
- Adjustment,
- Adjusted staff months,
- Optimal delivery time,
- Final staff months,
- Final cost,
- Final optimal delivery time, and
- Average cost per hour.

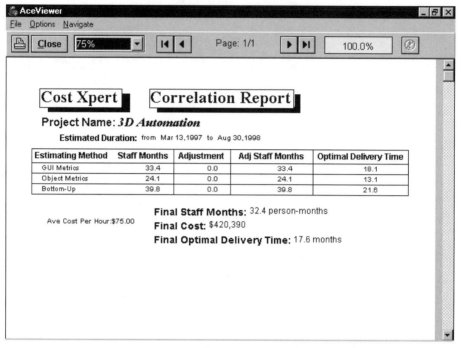

FIGURE 85 CORRELATION REPORT

TASKS

The Tasks report is displayed in Figure 86. This report displays the following field information:

- Task ID,
- Task,
- Deliverables,
- Percent,
- Cost,
- Duration, and
- Total cost.

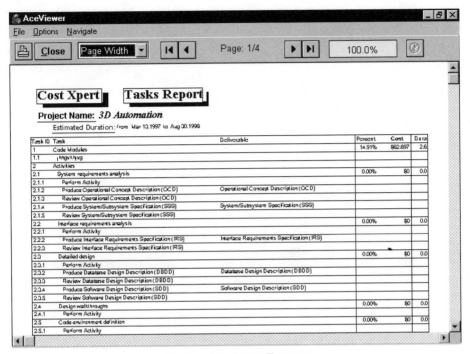

FIGURE 86 TASKS REPORT

RISK

The Risk report is displayed in Figure 87. This report displays the following field information:

- Likely risks, and
- Other risks.

  Environmental sensitivity analysis includes:

- Factor,
- Current value, and
- Possible impact.

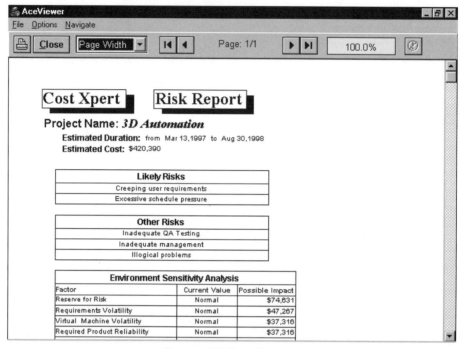

FIGURE 87 RISK REPORT

Risk tolerance comparisons include:

- Sigma,
- Final cost, and
- Duration.

LABOR

The Labor report is displayed in Figure 88. This report displays the following field information for the estimated required number for full-time staff:

- Month,
- Requirements analysis,
- Product designing,

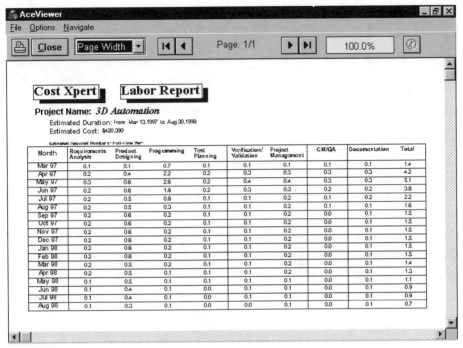

FIGURE 88 LABOR REPORT

- Programming,
- Test planning,
- Verification and validation,
- Project management,
- CM/QA,
- Documentation, and
- Total.

MAINTENANCE

The Labor report is displayed in Figure 89. This report displays the following fields:

- Inflation,
- Annual change traffic,

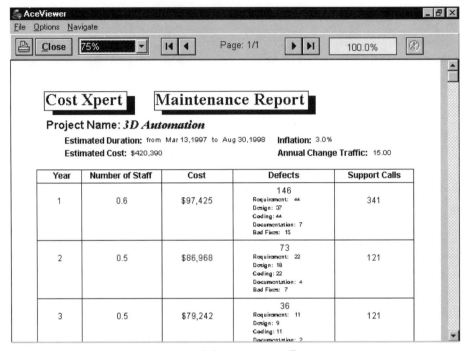

FIGURE 89 MAINTENANCE REPORT

- Year,
- Number of staff, and
- Cost.

Defects include:

- Requirement,
- Design,
- Coding,
- Documentation,
- Bad fixes, and
- Support calls.

DELIVERABLES

The Deliverables report is displayed in Figure 90. This report displays the following fields:

- Project standard,
- Deliverable name,
- Description, and
- Number of pages for document.

INPUT DATA

The Input Data report actually prints out seven separate reports containing information for your project.

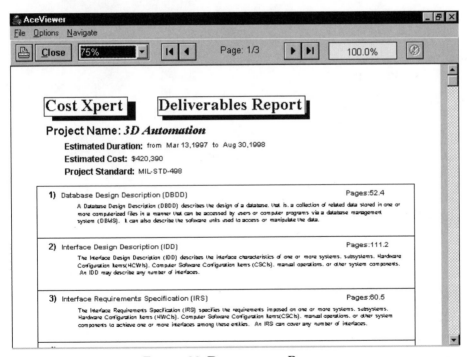

FIGURE 90 DELIVERABLES REPORT

Input Data, General Data

The Input Data, General Data report contains the following information:

- Project name,
- Project manager,
- Start date,
- End date,
- Duration,
- Company information, and
- Estimator information.

Miscellaneous information regarding the projects, including:

- Primary language,
- Secondary language,
- Coefficient,
- Life cycle,
- Average trip cost,
- Number of users,
- Average cost per hour,
- Total person months,
- Percent of code in primary language,
- Standard,
- Project type,
- Inflation factor,
- Annual change traffic, and
- Total cost.

Input Data, SLOC Data

The Input Data, SLOC Data report contains the following information:
SLOC data for new modules include:

- Best case,
- Expected case,
- Worst case,
- Mean, and
- Standard deviation.

SLOC data for reused modules includes:

- Module name,
- Actual LOC,
- Percent design,
- Percent code,
- Percent effort for I & T, and
- Equivalent LOC.

Input Data, Function Points Data

The Input Data, Function Points Data report contains the following information:

Function points data for new modules includes:

- Function point type,
- Best case,
- Worst case,
- Mean,
- Standard deviation, and
- Means total.

Function points data for reused modules includes:

- Function point type,
- Actual FPs,
- Percent design mods,
- Percent code mods,

- Percent effort for I & T,
- Equivalent LOC, and
- Equivalents total.

Input Data, GUI Metric Data

The Input Data, GUI Metric Data report contains the GUI metrics data for both the new and reused modules.

The GUI metrics data for new modules includes:

- GUI type,
- Best case,
- Expected case,
- Worst case,
- Mean, and
- Standard deviation.

The GUI metrics data for reused modules includes:

- GUI type,
- Actual GUIs,
- Percent design mods,
- Percent code mods,
- Percent effort for I & T, and
- Equivalent LOC.

Input Data, Object Metrics Data

The Input Data, Object Metrics Data report contains information for both new and reused modules.

Object Metrics data for new modules includes:

- Object type,
- Best case,
- Expected case,

- Worst case,
- Mean, and
- Standard Deviation.

  Object Metrics data for reused modules includes:

- Object type,
- Actual objects,
- Percent design mods,
- Percent code mods,
- Percent effort for I & T, and
- Equivalent LOC.

Input Data, Bottom Up Data

The Input Data, Bottom Up Data report contains the following information:

- Activity,
- Best,
- Expected,
- Worst,
- Mean,
- Standard Deviation,
- Expected Percentage,
- Typical Percentage, and
- Phase.

Input Data, Top Down Data

The Input Data, Top Down Data report contains the following information:

- Expected effort in person months,
- Activity,

- Typical Percentage,
- Typical effort,
- Estimated Percentage,
- Estimated effort, and
- Phase.

ALL

The Reports/All menu choice allows the user to print all reports for a selected project.

AD HOC

The Ad Hoc report menu choice allows a user to print custom reports in Cost•Xpert. The user can drop in fields from the database and customize reports to project needs.

RISK•XPERT

appendix

E

Risk•Xpert is a tool that supports both risk assessment and contingency planning and tracking to mitigate risks in a formal, optimized manner. Cost•Xpert can feed project-related risk factors directly into Risk•Xpert to serve as a starting point in your risk management activities. For more information on Risk•Xpert, contact *info@marotz.com* or visit *www.marotz.com.*

HyperText Standards On-Line

HyperText Standards On-Line (HTSO) is a powerful tool for working with software development standards. HTSO serves as a reference for anyone working with the various standards applicable to software development.

It includes all relevant standards used by:

- Department of Defense,
- Department of Energy,
- IEEE,
- Jet Propulsion Laboratory,
- ISO, and
- FIPS.

Standards include:

- DOD-STD-2167A,
- MIL-STD-498, and
- ISO 9000.

It provides a comprehensive database of standards in three different formats to meet a wide variety of needs:

1. On-line database with full keyword search capability,
2. Microsoft Help format, and
3. Word processor format.

The HTSO search engine allows a fast search and retrieval of standards, with full support for boolean and wildcard searches to quickly find any given subject. A comprehensive database of acronyms and technical terms is included so users can quickly look up a term and find the exact meaning, along with the source document.

Text versions of the government standards provide a starting point for technical staff when preparing deliverables, and the Microsoft Help compatible version of the standards can be linked to popular word processors, compilers, and CASE tools to allow the standards to be viewed directly within a user's development environment.

HTSO operates on an IBM PC compatible computer running Windows 95, Windows 3.1, Windows NT, or Windows 3.11.

appendix G

STRATEGY•XPERT

STRATEGIC OPTIMIZATION STEP-BY-STEP: PRIORITIZE YOUR MANAGEMENT DECISIONS

QFD Strategy•Xpert automatically guides you through the process of prioritizing your management decisions to optimally align your organization's strategic objectives.

Quality Function Deployment (QFD) Strategy•Xpert serves as a reference for anyone working with projects which have limited amounts of time, personnel, and financial resources. It allows the management team to best utilize its strengths with little or no waste of effectiveness.

Who Needs QFD Strategy•Xpert:

- Strategic planners developing strategic plans for organizations or information technology.
- Managers responsible for the allocation of scarce resources (e.g., people, money) between projects.
- Systems analysts and consultants looking for a valuable tool to support information engineering or business needs analysis.

QFD Strategy•Xpert allows you to compare actual versus optimal resource allocations, then store all strategic factors in a database. This allows you to easily maintain and update your strategic plan over time. It also works for a wide variety of optimization problems in addition to strategic planning; and with both hard copy and on-screen graphics, you can quickly and easily prepare reports and presentations.

Better use of resources means that revenue increases of 30% and cost reductions of 10% can be typically achieved.

Glossary Terms

Word	Description
Adaptive Maintenance	Adapting the software to handle changes in the environment, including changes to the operating system, database management system, and input files.
Allocating	Involves dividing the time and money among the phases, people, and tasks.
Analyst Capability	Measures the system engineer's capability as a team average.
Classified Application	Measures extra work required to develop software either in a classified security area, or for a classified security application.
Close Button	Button located at the top of the window on the upper right corner of Title bar. It closes the application window.
Computer Turnaround Time	Measures the time spent waiting for the development environment to complete the compi-

	lation and for the modified code to be ready for testing.
Corrective Maintenance	Correcting software defects (bugs).
Database Size	Determines the effects of the software development due to the size of the database that must be maintained and manipulated.
Dialog Boxes	Modal and non-modal dialog boxes such as popup data entry forms and tool palettes.
DLL	Acronym for Direct Link Library. These files may be required for Cost•Xpert to run properly.
Estimating	Involves determining the total cost and time required to complete the project.
Execution Time Constraints	Measures the approximate percentage of the available CPU execution time that will be used by the software in order to achieve the system's performance objectives.
External Inputs	Data entry screens or dialogs.
External Interface Files	Files that the system creates for use by other applications, and that other systems create for input into this application.
External Queries	On-line transactions from other systems that must be handled by this system.
External Outputs	Queries that involve reading data without updates.
GUI	Graphical User Interface.
Language Experience	Measures the design and programming team's experience with the programming language that will be used to design and implement the software.
Logical Internal Tables	Relational tables or other storage files used by the system.
Maximize Button	Button on the right side of the Caption Bar that allows a window to be maximized (dis-

	played full screen) or displayed in standard, overlapped mode.
Main Storage Constraints	Measures the amount of constraint imposed on the software due to main memory limitations in the target computer.
MDI	Microsoft's Multiple Document Interface Window Interface.
Menu Bar	Located at the top of the window just below the Title Bar. This bar displays the various menu choices available within Cost•Xpert.
Menu Choices	Number of unique menu choices in the application.
Menu Hot Keys	Function keys that allow a user to access a menu choice using the keyboard. These menu choices can be accessed by either pressing the Alt or Ctrl key simultaneously with the underlined letter in the desired menu choice.
Microsoft Help	The standard Windows help engine built into Windows. When you display help for virtually any Windows application, you are using the Microsoft Help engine.
Minimize button	Button to the left of the Maximize button on the Caption Bar. It allows a window to be minimized to an icon.
Modern Programming Practices	Quantifies the use of modern programming practices such as structured design, object-oriented design, formal data design methodologies, etc.
Percent Code Modification	Measures how much coding and unit testing effort will be saved by reused code.
Percent Design Modification	Measures how much design effort will be saved by reused code.
Percent Integration and Test	Measures how much integration and testing effort will be saved by reused code.

Perfective Maintenance	Making improvements in the software's functionality, usability, reliability, performance, or security.
Program Volume	Methods of estimating the size of a program.
Programming Team Capability	Measures the capability of the programmers who will actually perform the detailed design and write/test the physical code during coding and unit testing phases.
Project Application Experience	Measures the familiarity of the design and development team with this specific application area.
Readme File	The Readme.txt contains information and answers to questions that were too new for inclusion in the hard copy documentation. This file also contains a list of directories and files Cost•Xpert loads on your computer.
Required Reusability	Measures the extra effort needed to generalize software modules when they must be developed specifically for reuse in other software programs.
Required Software Reliability	Measures the required reliability of the finished software.
Requirement Volatility	Measures amount of project design and development rework that is the result of changes in customer specified requirements.
Reports	System reports.
SDI	Microsoft's Single Document Interface Window Interface.
SETUP.EXE	Installation program located on Disk #1 of distribution diskettes. Installs the Cost•Xpert application.
Software Product Complexity	Quantifies the complexity of the software product that is to be developed.

Software Tools	Measures use of automated software tools such as computer aided software engineering (CASE), the Ada programming support environment, integrated team development and test environments, etc.
System Menu Request Button	Button located at top of the window on the left corner of the Title Bar. This button provides access to standard Windows functions.
Tables	Number of logical relational tables in the system.
Title Bar	Bar at the top of a window containing the window's title, a System Menu Request, the Minimize button, the Maximize button, and the Close button.
Virtual Machine Experience	Measures the design and programming team's experience with the virtual machine.
Virtual Machine Volatility	Measures the amount of changes the virtual machine is expected to have during the design and development phases.
Windows	Number of independent windows in the system.

BIBLIOGRAPHY

[Balzer, 1983] Balzer, R., Cheatham, T. E., and Green, C., *Software Technology in the 1990s: Using a New Paradigm.* November, 1983, pp. 39–45.

[Boehm, 1981] Boehm, B., *Software Engineering Economics.* Englewood Cliffs, New Jersey: Prentice Hall, 1981.

[Boehm, 1987] Boehm, B., *Software Engineering and Project Management.* IEEE Press, 1987.

[Charette, 1989] Charette, R., *Software Engineering Risk Analysis and Management.* McGraw-Hill, 1989, p. 18.

[Conte, 1986] Conte, S., Dunsmore, H., and Shen, V., *Software Engineering Metrics and Models.* New York: Benjamin/Cummings, 1986.

[DeMarco, 1982] DeMarco, T., *Controlling Software Projects—Management, Measurement, and Estimation.* New York: Yourdon Press, 1982.

[Deutsch, 1990] Deutsch, M., *Scenario Oriented Engineering for Software Intensive Systems,* Proceedings of the PNWSQC, 1990, pp. 373–379.

[Dorfman, 1990] Dorfman, M., *System and Software Requirements.* IEEE Press, 1990.

[Freiman, 1979] Freiman, F. and Park, R., "Price software model version 3: An overview," in *Proc. IEEE-PINY Workshop Quantitative Software Models*, October 1979, pp. 32–41.

[Fugate, 1991] Fugate, C., "Estimating the cost of object-oriented programming," unpublished paper distributed to users of GE PRICE Software Model (PRICE S).

[Jensen, 1984] Jensen, R., "A comparison of the Jensen and COCOMO schedule and cost estimation models," in *Proc. International Society of Parametric Analysis*, 1984, pp. 96–106.

[Jones, 1989] Jones, C., *U.S. Industry Averages for Software Productivity and Quality*, Version 4.0. Burlington, Massachusetts: Software Productivity Research, Inc., 1989.

[Jones, 1991] Jones, C., *Applied Software Measurement—Assuring Productivity and Quality*. New York: McGraw-Hill, 1991.

[Laranjeira, 1990] Laranjeira, L., "Software size estimation of object-oriented systems," *IEEE Transactions on Software Engineering*, Vol. 16, No. 5 (May 1990), pp. 510–522.

[Manley, 1990] Manley, J., *The Dual Lifecycle Model: An Enterprise Perspective of Software Development, System and Software Requirements Engineering*. IEEE Press, 1990, pp. 505–512.

[McCabe, 1976] McCabe, T., "A Complexity Measure," *IEEE Transactions on Software Engineering*, December 1976, pp. 308–320.

[McCracken, 1982] McCracken, D. and Jackson, M., *Lifecycle Concept Considered Harmful*, Software Engineering Notes, ACM April 1982, pp. 29–32.

[Ness, 1988] Ness, B., "Analysis of software data collection and REVIC projects," *Hq AFCMD Technical Report* (October 1988). Available from REVIC Users Group, George Trever, Sandia National Laboratories, Organization 9215, Albuquerque, NM 87185-5800.

[Norden, 1970] Norden, P., "Useful Tools for Project Management," *Management of Production*, M.K. Starr, Ed.. Baltimore, Maryland: Penguin Books, 1970.

[Parr, 1980] Parr, F.,"An alternative to the Rayleigh Curve Model for Software Development Effort," *IEEE Transactions on Software Engineering,* May 1980, pp. 291–296.

[Pfleeger, 1991] Pfleeger, S.,"Model of software effort and productivity," *Information and Software Technology,* Vol. 33, No. 3 (April 1991), pp. 224–231.

[Putnam, 1978] Putnam, L.,"A general empirical solution to the macro software sizing and estimation problem," *IEEE Transactions on Software Engineering,* Vol. SE-4, No. 4 (July 1978), pp. 345–361.

[Roetzheim, 1991] Roetzheim, W., *Developing Software to Government Standards.* Englewood Cliffs, New Jersey: Prentice Hall, 1991.

[Walston, 1977] Walston, C. and Felix, C., "A method of programming measurement and estimation," *IBM Systems Journal,* Vol. 16, No. 1 (1977), pp. 54–73.

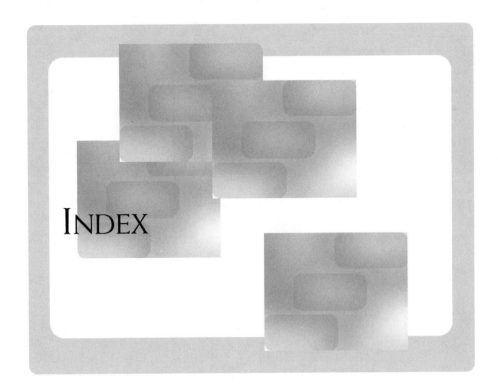

INDEX

About the Software

FREE SOFTWARE

The CD-Rom disc contains free evaluation copies of three Windows-based estimating and scheduling software tools: Cost•Expert™, Risk•Expert™, and Strategy•Expert.™

While it is possible to do effective cost and schedule estimating using nothing more complicated than a series of paper forms and a spreadsheet program, there are powerful computer programs available to simplify the task. One of the newest and most powerful Windows-based costing tools available today is Cost•Xpert. This tool supports cost and schedule estimating using lines of code, function points, GUI metrics, object metrics, and other techniques. It features a comprehensive set of environmental adjustments, adjusts costs based on various project constraints, and supports integrated risk assessment.

Cost•Xpert was calibrated using over 2,000 projects, including a wide mixture of commercial, military, and scientific projects. It accurately predicts project costs within ± 5% given accurate inputs, and compares within ± 2% to popular estimating tools costing $50,000 to $200,000.

Cost•Xpert runs under Windows 95 or Windows NT and requires a 486 or higher machine. Cost•Xpert is also available for downloading from *www.marotz.com*. This version works using a local stand-alone database, but client-server versions of Cost•Xpert are available supporting a variety of databases, including SQL Server. For more information about purchasing a fully functional version of Cost•Xpert or the client-server version, refer to____of this book or contact Marotz directly at (800) 477-6168.

GUARANTEE

Our liabilities shall be limited solely to replacement discs and documentation and shall not include any other damages. We will not be liable for consequential, indirect, special, or other similar damages or claims, including loss of profits or any other commercial damage. In no event will Marotz, Inc.'s liability for damages to you or any other person ever exceed the price paid for the license to use the program.

LIMITED WARRANTY

Marotz, Inc. warrants the physical program discs and physical documentation to be free of defects in materials and workmanship for a period of sixty (60) days from the date of purchase.

LICENSE AGREEMENT

Cost•Xpert is not copy protected, but it is protected by copyright law and international treaty provisions.

LICENSE AGREEMENT AND LIMITED WARRANTY

READ THE FOLLOWING TERMS AND CONDITIONS CAREFULLY BEFORE OPENING THIS CD PACKAGE. THIS LEGAL DOCUMENT IS AN AGREEMENT BETWEEN YOU AND PRENTICE-HALL INC. (THE "COMPANY"). BY OPENING THIS SEALED CD PACKAGE, YOU ARE AGREEING TO BE BOUND BY THESE TERMS AND CONDITIONS. IF YOU DO NOT AGREE WITH THESE TERMS AND CONDITIONS, DO NOT OPEN THE CD PACKAGE. PROMPTLY RETURN THE UNOPENED CD PACKAGE AND ALL ACCOMPANYING ITEMS TO THE PLACE YOU OBTAINED THEM FOR A FULL REFUND OF ANY SUMS YOU HAVE PAID.

1.　　**GRANT OF LICENSE:** In consideration of your purchase of this book, and your agreement to abide by the terms and conditions of this Agreement, the Company grants to you a nonexclusive right to use and display the copy of the enclosed software program (hereinafter the "SOFTWARE") on as single computer (i.e., with a single CPU) at a single location so long as you comply with the terms of this agreement. The Company reserves all rights not expressly granted to you under this Agreement.

2.　　**OWNERSHIP OF SOFTWARE:** You own only the magnetic or physical media (the enclosed CD) on which the SOFTWARE is recorded or fixed, but the Company and the software developers retain all the rights, title, and ownership to the SOFTWARE recorded on the original CD copy(ies) and all subsequent copies of the SOFTWARE, regardless of the form or media on which the original or other copies may exist. This license is not a sale of the original SOFTWARE or any copy to you.

3.　　**COPY RESTRICTIONS:** This SOFTWARE and the accompanying printed materials and user manual (the "Documentation") are the subject of the copyright. The individual programs on the CD are copyrighted by the authors of each program. You may not copy the Documentation or the SOFTWARE, except that you may make a single copy of the SOFTWARE for backup or archival purposes only. You may be held legally responsible for any copying or copyright infringement which is caused or encouraged by your failure to abide by the terms of this restriction.

4.　　**USE RESTRICTIONS:** You may not network the SOFTWARE or otherwise use it on more than one computer or computer terminal at the same time. You may physically transfer the SOFTWARE from one computer to another provided that the SOFTWARE is used on only one computer at at time. You may not distribute copies of the SOFTWARE or Documentation to others. You may not reverse engineer, disassemble, modify, adapt, translate, or create derivative works based on the SOFTWARE or the Documentation without prior written consent of the Company.

5.　　**TRANSFER RESTRICTIONS:** The enclosed SOFTWARE is licensed only to you and may not be transferred to any one else without the prior written consent of the Company. Any unauthorized transfer of the SOFTWARE shall result in the immediate termination of this Agreement.

6.　　**TERMINATION:** This license is effective until terminated. This license will terminate automatically without notice form the Company and become null and void if you fail to comply with any provisions or limitations of this license. Upon termination, you shall destroy the Documentation and all copies of the SOFTWARE. All provisions of this Agreement as to warranties, limitation of liability, remedies or damages, and our ownership shall survive termination.

7.　　**MISCELLANEOUS:** This Agreement shall be construed in accordance with the laws of the United States of American and the State of New York and shall benefit the Company, its affiliates, and assignees.

8.　　**LIMITED WARRANTY AND DISCLAIMER OF WARRANTY:**　The Company warrants that the SOFTWARE, when properly used in accordance with the Documentation, will operate in substantial conformity with the description of the SOFTWARE set forth in the Documentation. The Company does not warrant that the SOFTWARE will meet your requirements or that the operation of the SOFTWARE will be uninterrupted or error-free. The Company warrants that the media on which the SOFTWARE is delivered shall be free from defects in materials and workmanship under normal use for a period of thirty (30) days from the date of your purchase. Your only remedy and the Company's only obligation under these limited warranties is, at the Company's option, return of the warranted item for a refund of amounts paid by you or replacement of the item. Any replacement of SOFTWARE or media under the warranties shall not apply to any SOFTWARE which the Company determines in good faith has been subject to misuse, neglect, improper installation, repair, alteration, or damage by you. EXCEPT FOR THE EXPRESSED WARRANTIES SET FORTH ABOVE, THE COMPANY DISCLAIMS ALL WARRANTIES, EXPRESS OR IMPLIED, INCLUDING WITHOUT LIMITATION, THE IMPLIED WARRANTIES OF MERCHANTABILITY AND FITNESS FOR A PARTICULAR PURPOSE. EXCEPT FOR THE EXPRESS WARRANTY SET FORTH ABOVE, THE COMPANY DOES NOT WARRANT, GUARANTEE, OR MAKE ANY REPRESENTATION REGARDING THE USE OR RESULTS OF THE SOFTWARE IN TERMS OF ITS CORRECTNESS, ACCURACY, RELIABILITY, CURRENTNESS OR OTHERWISE.

IN NO EVENT, SHALL THE COMPANY OR ITS EMPLOYEES, AGENTS, SUPPLIERS, OR CONTRACTORS BE LIABLE FOR ANY INCIDENTAL, INDIRECT, SPECIAL, OR CONSEQUENTIAL DAMAGES ARISING OUT OF OR IN CONNECTION WITH THE LICENSE GRANTED UNDER THIS AGREEMENT, OR FOR LOSS OF USE, LOSS OF DATA, LOSS OF INCOME OR PROFIT, OR OTHER LOSSES, SUSTAINED AS A RESULT OF INJURY TO ANY PERSON, OR LOSS OF OR DAMAGE TO PROPERTY, OR CLAIMS OF THIRD PARTIES, EVEN IF THE COMPANY OR AN AUTHORIZED REPRESENTATIVE OF THE COMPANY HAS BEEN ADVISED OF THE POSSIBILITY OF SUCH DAMAGES. IN NO EVENT SHALL LIABILITY OF THE COMPANY FOR DAMAGES WITH RESPECT TO THE SOFTWARE EXCEED THE AMOUNTS ACTUALLY PAID BY YOU, IF ANY, FOR THE SOFTWARE.

SOME JURISDICTIONS DO NOT ALLOW THE LIMITATION OF IMPLIED WARRANTIES OR LIABILITY FOR INCIDENTAL, INDIRECT, SPECIAL, OR CONSEQUENTIAL DAMAGES, SO THE ABOVE LIMITATIONS MAY NOT ALWAYS APPLY. THE WARRANTIES IN THIS AGREEMENT GIVE YOU SPECIFIC LEGAL RIGHTS AND YOU MAY ALSO HAVE OTHER RIGHTS WHICH VARY IN ACCORDANCE WITH LOCAL LAW.

ACKNOWLEDGMENT

YOU ACKNOWLEDGE THAT YOU HAVE READ THIS AGREEMENT, UNDERSTAND IT, AND AGREE TO BE BOUND BY ITS TERMS AND CONDITIONS. YOU ALSO AGREE THAT THIS AGREEMENT IS THE COMPLETE AND EXCLUSIVE STATEMENT OF THE AGREEMENT BETWEEN YOU AND THE COMPANY AND SUPERSEDES ALL PROPOSALS OR PRIOR AGREEMENTS, ORAL, WRITTEN, AND ANY OTHER COMMUNICATION BETWEEN YOU AND THE COMPANY OR ANY OTHER COMMUNICATIONS BETWEEN YOU AND THE COMPANY OR ANY REPRESENTATIVE OF THE COMPANY RELATING TO THE SUBJECT MATTER OF THIS AGREEMENT

Should you have any questions concerning this Agreement or if you wish to contact the Company for any reason, please contact in writing at the address below:

Robin Short
Prentice Hall PTR
One Lake Street
Upper Saddle River, New Jersey 07458